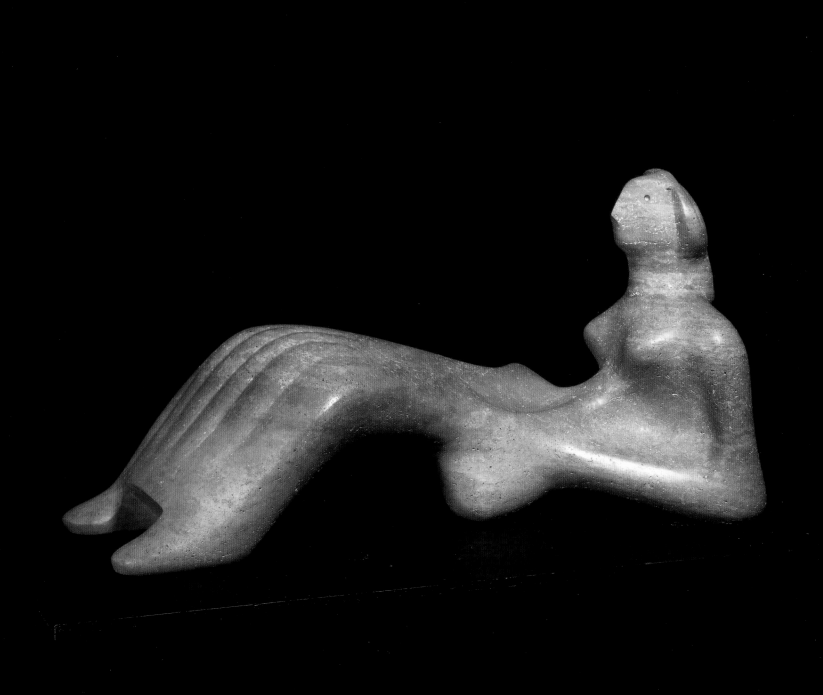

SOTHEBY'S
ART AT AUCTION

1996–1997

First published in 1997 by
Sotheby's
34–35 New Bond Street
London W1A 2AA

British Library Cataloguing in
Publication Data

A catalogue record for this
book is available from the
British Library.

ISBN 0-9622588-4-9

Project Editor: Emma Lawson

Copy Editors: Kate Quarry,
Kate Bouverie

Associate Editor: Lynn Stowell
Pearson

Production Controller:
Chris Smith

Art Editor: Sally Jeffery,
Jeffery Design

Art Director: Ruth Blacksell

Printed in Germany by
Mohndruck, Gütersloh

Endpapers: Ming and Qing
porcelain from a private
collection, see p. 35

Half-title: Henry Moore,
Reclining Figure – Bone Skirt,
1978, travertine marble, length
175 cm (69 in), New York
$2,202,500 (£1,342,987)
13.v.97

Frontispiece: Canaletto, *Interior
View of the Henry VII Chapel,
Westminster Abbey*, early 1750s,
oil on canvas, 77.5 × 67 cm
(30½ × 26¼ in), London
£771,500 ($1,303,835) 6.VII.97

Page 255: A Mixtec Gold
Pendant of a Deity
Monte Alban, Early
Postclassic, *c.* AD 900–1250
Height 5.7 cm (2¼ in)
New York $79,500 (£47,326)
25.XI.96

CONTENTS

INTRODUCTION

Diana D. Brooks

Diana D. Brooks is President and Chief Executive Officer, Board of Directors, Sotheby's Holdings, Inc.

If the 1996–97 auction season at Sotheby's left one abiding impression it was that collectors will go to any lengths to acquire art of the highest quality. During the year a number of truly wonderful works in a broad range of collecting areas were offered in our salerooms throughout the world, with many achieving record prices. Looking back, one sees that the character of the entire auction season was, in large measure, defined by new price levels that were achieved for those works that represented the ultimate in quality and rarity.

I can think of no better example than our cover image. Vincent van Gogh's panoramic view of Arles, *La Moisson en Provence*, was executed by the artist in 1888 and has long been regarded as one of his greatest watercolours (see p. 74). Acquired in 1924 by its late owner, the distinguished British collector Mrs J. B. A. Kessler, the painting had been exhibited publicly only once during the past half a century. Its appearance in our June sale of Impressionist and Modern Art in London – which also included the fine Tabachnick Collection of Fauve and Expressionist Art – caused great excitement. This masterpiece achieved £8,801,500 ($14,698,505), making it the most expensive modern picture to be sold in any European auction since 1990.

As the pages of this book reveal, the season brought with it many successes in such other collecting fields as Old Master Paintings, Asian Art, Western Manuscripts, American Paintings and Silver. We hope that this pictorial review will provide a window on the many exciting moments of the past year at Sotheby's.

Litzlbergerkeller am Attersee (detail) by Gustav Klimt set a world auction record for the artist when it sold at Sotheby's New York for $14,742,500 (£9,140,350) on 13 May 1997 (see p. 79).

SOTHEBY'S YEAR IN EUROPE

Simon de Pury and
Henry Wyndham

Simon de Pury is Chairman, Board of Sotheby's Holdings, Sotheby's Europe and Sotheby's Switzerland. **Henry Wyndham** is Chairman of Sotheby's UK.

The very nature of an auction encompasses breathtaking drama, excitement and surprise – all of which could describe the 1996–97 season at Sotheby's in London and Europe. Whilst high points were created by the breaking of a considerable number of world auction records, the season also witnessed a pleasing strengthening of Sotheby's position within the market-place, achieved through a winning combination of departmental expertise and works of remarkable quality and provenance. Sotheby's sales turned over significantly more from September 1996 to July 1997 than in the previous season, even in the absence of a large single-owner sale such as the Grand Ducal Collections of Baden, with the Impressionist and Modern Art, Old Master Paintings and British Paintings sales producing figures that had not been achieved for almost ten years. Such a breadth of strong results is cause for celebration.

Outside the saleroom, Sotheby's London headquarters in New Bond Street followed up the success of last January's exhibition, *The Artist and the Country House*, with an equally fascinating collection of work celebrating three centuries of trade between Canton, Shanghai, Hong Kong and Europe, entitled *A Tale of Three Cities*. The exhibition, the first of its kind to cover such a wide field, encompassed more than 300 carefully chosen, diverse objects, which were displayed in the form of a journey taken by the great merchant ships. Coincidentally, the strength of the market for Chinese export works of art was borne out by the price achieved for a biscuit figure of a tiger sold the previous November (see p. 155). New Bond Street also saw the establishment of The Café as one of the most written about and popular new restaurants in London. As A. A. Gill wrote in the *Sunday Times*, 'Service was charming . . . It's all done with immaculately good taste; it's unpretentious but smart, the menu is well within the capacity of the kitchen and staff.'

During the year, Sotheby's achieved world records for an extraordinary range of items, some of the most remarkable of which included a Parahi painting (£166,500, see p. 136), a Dutch Book of Hours from the Beck Collection (£1,002,500, see p. 135), a British watercolour (£826,500, *far right*), a stainless steel watch (£573,500, see p. 220), a print of an Edward Weston photograph (£110,500, see p. 33) and John Lennon's handwritten lyrics to 'Being For the Benefit Of Mr Kite!' (£66,400, see p. 243). Records for individual artists included Gerard ter Borch (£2,751,500, see p. 51), Jacques-Louis David (£3,741,500, see p. 65), a work on paper by Vincent van Gogh (£8,801,500, see pp. 74–75), Antonio Joli (£969,500, see p. 56) and Lucien Pissarro (£430,500, *right*).

World auction records are often achieved by works that have been previously thought lost, destroyed or even not to exist at all. The identification of a missing masterpiece – with the accompanying suggestions of obscurity, detective work and rediscovery – bestows an unusual provenance on a piece, frequently adding to its value. Nowhere is the skill of departmental specialists more apparent than in this area, and the 1996–97 season was marked by some exceptional finds. Christopher de Hamel, head of the Western Manuscripts department at Sotheby's London, instantly recognized a long-lost fragment from a magnificent gradual in the monastery of Santa Maria degli Angeli when it was brought to the Sotheby's valuation counter. Its owner had no idea of its identity or value; it had hung on her drawing-room wall for 'as long as [she] could remember'. Offered for sale on 17 June 1997 it reached a price of £84,000 (see p. 133). Another extraordinary find was made by Sotheby's expert Kerry Taylor when she identified a velvet purse as being that which held the Great Seal of England during the reign of Elizabeth I. Discovered in a trunk where it had lain for years, Sotheby's traced the purse

to a Welsh auction in 1890, thence back to Sir Thomas Egerton, Elizabeth I's Lord Keeper, and finally to Henry Jones, who was in Egerton's entourage. The purse was sold by private treaty to the British Museum, where it was instantly placed on display. The London Old Master Paintings sale on 3 July 1997 was marked by high excitement when Frans Hals' long-lost fourth Evangelist from a set acquired by Catherine the Great in 1760 came up for sale. Estimated at £300,000–400,000, the painting sold for £1,926,500 (see p. 50).

The season also witnessed innovations in the departmentalizing of items into themed sales, a development that Sotheby's has pioneered. Fast becoming an institution, the Irish Sale returned for its third successive – and successful – year. Much of its success is due not only to the range of items included in the sale – from paintings and furniture to ceramics and books – but also to the national context in which these items are placed, with a high percentage of the lots returning to Ireland. Continuing this concept, October welcomed the first Turkish Sale to the London salerooms. Casting its net to encompass works of art,

miniatures, textiles and European paintings, this event introduced a large number of new buyers to the market, whose interest in mid-range objects sent prices leaping above their pre-sale estimates. The subject of the sale seemed peculiarly timely in a year in which the Orient featured prominently as a motif in paintings by Eugène Delacroix (see p. 67), John Frederick Lewis (see p. 61) and Jean-Léon Gérôme (see p. 70), amongst others.

Following a month later was the Racing Sale. Brainchild of the Marquess of Hartington, Deputy Chairman of Sotheby's, this was a wonderful collection of all things connected with racing and more than lived up to its subtitle, *A Celebration of the Turf*. Opening with a series of striking portraits of racehorses, their riders and owners by artists such as James Seymour, John Frederick Herring, Snr and Ben Marshall, the sale went on to include sculpture, ceramics, books, silver, even silks and the registering of new silks. In a packed saleroom prices soared and 93 per cent of the lots were sold.

The autumn saw a number of exciting sales take place in Sotheby's European locations. The legendary

Lilium Auratum by John Frederick Lewis RA (above) set a new world record for a British watercolour when it achieved a price of £826,500 ($1,380,255) on 20 November 1996. This work, the Latin title of which translates as 'the gilded lily', shows an odalisque and her servant gathering flowers in the walled garden of a harem.

The Tomatoes (above left) is both an extremely rare example of Lucien Pissarro's earliest work, showing his roots in the mainstream of French Impressionism, and also a very unusual instance of a still life by him. Included in the sale of Modern British Art from a Private Collection in June, this work set a new world auction record for a painting by the artist when it sold for £430,500 ($701,715).

Property from the Collections of the Earls of Warwick appeared in a number of sales throughout the season, provenance and quality leading to significantly high prices. On 5 June 1997 this pair of Charles II silver-gilt vases (58.5 cm/23 in high) by Arthur Manwaring sold for £243,500 ($399,340), more than four times their lower pre-sale estimate.

This Ottoman painted room c. 1800 was a dramatic addition to the Turkish Sale held in London on 11 October 1996. With a pre-sale estimate of £60,000–80,000, the interior reached a final price of £199,500 ($313,215).

collection of dolls belonging to Dina Vierny, muse of French sculptor Aristide Maillol and model to Henri Matisse, was auctioned in the London salerooms on 17–18 October. Considered to be the most important collection of such items in existence, the sale took a total of over £2.4 million ($3.8 million, see p. 245). In November, Amsterdam played host to the collection of HRH Princess Christina of the Netherlands, younger sister of Queen Beatrix. Distinguished both by royal provenance and rich diversity, the sale attracted considerable interest and was 98 per cent sold with a number of lots going way over their estimates. On 20 November the ultimate collection of jewellery by the great Art Nouveau artist René Lalique was sold at Sotheby's Geneva. These exquisite pieces were characterized by inspired imagination, sophisticated draughtsmanship and the highest standards of technical virtuosity, confirming Lalique as one of the most masterful designers of his time (*opposite, left*).

Sotheby's continental furniture sales traditionally carry the title French Furniture; Mario Tavella, head of the London department, made a break with tradition for his December sale, incorporating 'Italian' into the title in tribute to a number of outstanding pieces that formed a rare group to come to auction at one time. The appropriateness of this decision was more than justified by the results, with the star of the sale, a

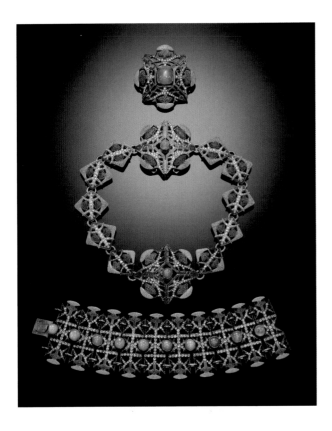

walnut, burr-walnut and parcel-gilt bureau cabinet, reaching a price of £540,000 (see p. 191). Days later, Monaco auctioned treasures from the French royal family that had furnished Quinta de Anjinho, the home in exile of the Comte and Comtesse de Paris during the 1940s. Pre-sale estimates were far exceeded; a crystal glassware service engraved with the arms and monogram of the Duc d'Aumale, estimated at FF20,000–30,000, sold for FF594,900 (£69,008; $114,221). A sapphire, diamond and pearl parure from this collection, which had once belonged to Marie-Amélie, Queen of the French, was sold separately in Geneva on 21 May 1997 (see p. 212). Achieving a price of SF1,378,500, this group was a fitting climax to a glittering sale. In honour of his contribution to the diamond trade, David Bennett – Director of Sotheby's Jewellery and Precious Objects Division, Europe and Deputy Chairman of Sotheby's Switzerland – was this year awarded the prestigious Antwerp Diamond Career Award 1997 by the Diamond High Council.

Back in London the season reached its climax with a succession of groundbreaking results. The Beck Collection of Illuminated Manuscripts consisted of only thirty-four lots, yet their quality, beauty and history – numbering two saints, a queen and a Holy Roman Emperor amongst their first owners – took the sale's total to £11,158,415 ($18,299,801). Auction records were

set for four artists during the Modern British and Irish Paintings sale on 18 June, including Victor Pasmore (see p. 63) and William Scott (see p. 62). The evening sale of Impressionist and Modern Art, which included one of Vincent van Gogh's greatest watercolours (see pp. 74–75) and Fauve and Expressionist Art from the Collection of Charles Tabachnick (see pp. 30–31 and 83–85), achieved results of over £34.5 million ($58.3 million), the highest total for such a sale in Europe since 1990. The overall total for the two-day sale was £42,348,842 ($70,799,900). Two days later the sale of Contemporary Art took a total of over £7 million ($11.6 million). Into July, and the results kept coming. The Old Master Paintings sale made £19,246,325 ($32,333,826), set two world auction records and had five lots selling above the £1 million mark. Finally, less than a week later, two masterpieces by Antonio Joli (see p. 56), a beautiful Canaletto (see p. 2) and a series of paintings by the Master of the Tumbled Chairs in the British Paintings 1500–1850 sale ensured that the season ended on a high note, achieving a total of over £5 million ($8.5 million).

We hope that this relatively small selection of highlights from the 1996–97 season at Sotheby's captures the breadth and quality of the auctions that take place in our salerooms across Europe, and we look ahead to the next season, when we will be building upon the success already achieved.

The Minami Art Museum collection of breathtaking jewellery by *fin de siècle* artist René Lalique was just one of the high points in Geneva's jewellery sales. The Thistle Suite (above left) sold for SF399,500 (£188,564; $314,407).

The sale of *Susanna al bagno* by Italian artist Francesco Hayez (above) sent ripples of excitement around the Milan saleroom when its price soared to L1,199,100,000 (£431,796; $708,146), setting a new auction record for the artist.

SOTHEBY'S YEAR IN NORTH AMERICA | Richard Oldenburg

The 1996–97 auction season at Sotheby's, New York achieved record prices in widely diverse fields – from American painting to French silver, from Chinese furniture to movie posters. New highs for individual artists at auction were set by works dating from the seventeenth century through recent decades of the twentieth. A strong, discriminating market was evident in all collecting areas, and buyers were quite willing to pay extraordinary prices for extraordinary quality.

The Asia Week sales in September 1996 presented an outstanding assemblage of works. A horseshoe-back armchair (see p. 154) with great purity of design set a new record for Chinese furniture at auction. Another exceptional piece in the sale of Chinese works was a 'Hundred Deer' vase, a masterpiece of porcelain enamel technique from the eighteenth century Quianlong period (p. 14). The sale of Japanese works of art was highlighted by six sections of a rare seventeenth-century set of Japanese paintings (see p. 157), reunited after forty years in separate collections, which attracted vigorous bidding. The total for the Asia Week series of sales was $11.5 million (£7.36 million).

November is traditionally the height of the autumn auction season in New York, with the greatly anticipated Impressionist and Modern and Contemporary Art sales. Although only one segment – however major – of the large and diverse collecting world, these sales are often viewed as barometers of the strength of the art market as a whole, closely watched by the press and art community. The soaring values placed on individual works, the prominence of potential bidders, wide media coverage and other factors all combine to lend a special excitement to these events each season. With exceptional works from the Shelburne Museum (see pp. 26–27) and other collections, the autumn Impressionist and Modern Art sale was a memorable event, both for the distinction of the works included and for the level of prices achieved. The total for the two-part sale was $110.89 million (£67.6 million), with two works selling for more than $10 million, and seven for more than $5 million. As an indication of the recovered strength of the current market, two of the top works brought prices higher than they had achieved in sales at the market's remarkable height in 1989–90.

The autumn sale of Contemporary Art achieved a total of $17.3 million (£10.4 million), led by works by Roy Lichtenstein and Cy Twombly. Five artists' records were established for works by Eva Hesse, Walter de Maria, William Wiley, Cindy Sherman and Mike Kelley.

One of the landmark events of the autumn season took place in a different field from painting and sculpture – the landmark sale in November of Royal French Silver, the Property of George Ortiz, which brought $15.3 million (£9.3 million), nearly twice the highest total of any previous sale of silver at auction. A magnificent Louis XV Royal silver tureen, made in 1733 by Thomas Germain, sold for $10.3 million, a new record for a single silver piece at auction (see pp. 36–37).

The calendar year 1996 closed on a high note with the notably successful December sale of American Paintings, Drawings and Sculpture, which brought $34.2 million (£20.9 million), the largest total for a sale in this category since 1989. The outstanding work of the sale was Sargent's *Cashmere* (see pp. 28–29), while other highlights were Frederic Remington's *The Norther* (*opposite*), and a superb marble bust of Benjamin Franklin by Jean-Antoine Houdon (see p. 175). At $2.9 million the work set a record for Houdon at auction.

The new year was handsomely launched with an Old Master Paintings sale, in which prices soared to a total of $47.7 million (£29.6 million), setting a new record for a sale in this category. Highlighted by the inclusion of eight major paintings from the Saul P. Steinberg Collection and twenty-four works from the collection formed by the British Rail Pension Fund, the sale brought exceptional prices for works by Rembrandt (see p. 45) and Canaletto (see p. 46). Records at auction were set by six artists, including Frans Post and Michael Sweerts (see p. 49). Other January sales of special note included the several sessions of Important Americana. With a total of $18.2 million (£10.7 million), this was one of the strongest Americana sales series to date. Among its high points were a new record for a Newport highboy (see p. 186) and a record for a Shaker drawing at auction, *The Tree of Light* by Hannah Cohoon (see p. 184).

A moving event in January was the sale of works from the estate of the late Robert Woolley, Sotheby's beloved

Richard Oldenburg is Chairman of Sotheby's North America.

Frederic Remington's dramatic sculpture *The Norther* (opposite) was featured in the December American Paintings and Sculpture auction, selling for an impressive $3,632,500 (£2,215,852).

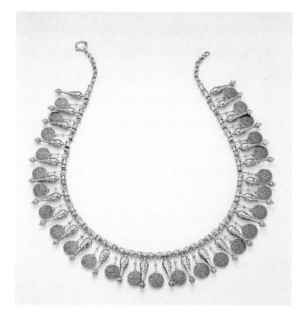

The 'Hundred Deer' vase (above), which achieved a price of $376,500 (£240,960) in September, is thought to symbolize high promotion or rank. The Chinese word for 'hundred deer', *bai lu*, is a pun referring to the number of deer or ranks; the word for both is *lu*.

The antique design of this striking gold and micro-mosaic necklace (right) by Castellani, *c.*1875, reflects the influence of archaeologist Michelangelo Caetani on its makers. Achieving a price of $13,800 (£8,459), it was one of the many beautiful pieces of jewellery sold in New York on 11 June.

and charismatic long-time director of Decorative Arts. As an auctioneer at numerous benefit events, Woolley raised many millions of dollars for philanthropic causes, including the fight against AIDS. Many of the works he had acquired – as a self-styled 'accumulator' rather than collector – were purchased by friends and colleagues as mementoes of their great affection and admiration for the owner, and the sale raised almost $1.5 million (£0.9 million) for various charities.

The spring sales in March devoted to the arts of Asia, proved to be the most successful series since the inception of Asia Week in 1992. The sale of Important Chinese Snuff Bottles brought over $1 million (£0.63 million), a record Sotheby's sale in this category, and the total of $3.7 million (£2.3 million) for the subsequent sale of Indian and South-East Asian works of art was the highest ever in its field. The sale of Chinese works of art ($6,254,317) was the strongest since the height of the market in 1989, highlighted by a Tang Dynasty unglazed pottery figure of a stallion (see p. 151). March also brought success in a quite different area, in the sale of the Feiertag Collection of Fine Movie Posters, which realized a total of $1.3 million (£0.8 million), a new record for a single sale of such posters. After a bidding contest among determined collectors a vintage poster from the 1932 classic horror film *The Mummy* (see p. 242) sold for the remarkable price of $453,500, more than twice the previous record for a movie poster at auction.

Two April auctions launched Sotheby's new Fashion department, recognizing the significance of *haute couture* as an art form and emblem of its time. The first was of property from the estate of Martha Phillips, the legendary creator of the Martha fashion empire, and the second presented *haute couture* by Scassi, the famed designer for clients like Elizabeth Taylor and Barbra Streisand, which was auctioned to benefit the Breast Cancer Research Foundation. The April sale of Magnificent Jewellery, which included the Martha Phillips Collection, achieved a total of over $25 million and set a new record price per carat for a yellow diamond.

As usual, the auction season reached a peak of interest and anticipation in May, with the spring sales of Contemporary, Impressionist and Modern, and Latin American Art. Of particular note was a strong sale of Contemporary Art, the first in New York to be assembled and conducted by Tobias Meyer, the newly appointed head of Sotheby's Worldwide Contemporary Art department. Carefully edited and paced, the sale included important works from the distinguished collection formed by the late William C. Janss, from the holdings of CBS Inc., and from the property of the Boston Children's Heart Foundation. While the top lots were works by classic modern masters like Franz Kline (see p. 88–89) and Mark Rothko (see p. 90), the enthusiastic response to challenging works by less established contemporary artists was particularly notable and encouraging for the future. Record prices at auction were set for five of these artists: Matthew Barney (see p. 97), Robert Gober, Jeff Koons, Kiki Smith and Rachel Whiteread. The total for the sale was $21.9 million (£13.4 million).

With important works from three major collections, those of Serge Sabarsky, of Florence and Richard Weil and of the artist Henry Moore, the two-part sale of Impressionist and Modern Art achieved a total of over $100 million (£62 million), highlighted by a luminous landscape by Gustav Klimt (see pp. 6 and 79), which set a record for the artist at $14.7 million. Subsequent spring sales continued to achieve record results. Latin American Art in May established new highs at auction for thirteen artists. American Indian Art in June achieved a record total for a sale in this field, as well as a record price for a single work of Indian art at auction. The sale of American Paintings, Drawings and Sculpture in June set new record prices for Andrew Wyeth (see p. 105) and ten other American artists.

Despite the impressive results achieved in other spring sales, for many auction-goers the most memorable event of the season was the sale, spread over three days, of more than 1,100 items from the estate of Ambassador Pamela Harriman. The property from Mrs Harriman's three residences reflected her life at the centre of political and diplomatic circles in London, Washington and Paris, and included paintings, furniture, decorations, books, silver, wine and historic memorabilia. More than 6,000 people attended the pre-sale exhibitions and nearly 5,000 absentee bids were recorded. With this high level of public interest and international press attention, the sale was a resounding success, bringing a total of $8.7 million (£5.3 million), far exceeding the pre-sale high estimate. A dramatic painting by John Singer Sargent, *Staircase in Capri* (*right*), achieved the highest price, but items of historical significance, like the pen used by President Kennedy to sign the Nuclear Test Ban Treaty, memorabilia such as a set of silver plates formerly owned by Winston Churchill, and purely decorative pieces all found eager purchasers, many of them first-time bidders at auction.

At the end of June the installation of Keith Haring's witty and playful large-scale sculptures along Park Avenue, arranged by the Public Art Fund in cooperation with the André Emmerich Gallery, a division of Sotheby's, welcomed summer and, with it, the close of another stimulating and highly successful season for Sotheby's New York.

Staircase in Capri by John Singer Sargent sold for $1,432,500 (£873,825) on 19 May. A work beautiful in its minimalism and deceptive simplicity, it formed part of the Estate of Ambassador Pamela Harriman.

Julian Thompson, Co-Chairman, Management Board, Sotheby's Asia, started the Hong Kong auctions in 1973.
Alice Lam joined Sotheby's Asia as Co-Chairman in 1996.

This rich emerald-green jadeite bangle, made from an unusually large stone, was a high point in Lisa Hubbard's jadeite jewellery sales, achieving a price of HK$9,590,000 (£767,200; $1,246,700).

For Sotheby's in Asia the 1996–97 season proved to be an eventful twelve months. After a distinguished career with the Hang Seng Bank in Hong Kong, Alice Lam joined me in mid 1996 as Co-Chairman of Sotheby's, Asia, and, by the end of the year, had masterminded the move of our Asian headquarters in Hong Kong to larger premises in an excellent new building at the western end of Central District. The new office has not only provided the space needed for an essential increase in staff to meet the challenges of an expanding Asian business, it also includes a small auction room which can be used for previewing exhibitions in house. The move also underlines our long-term commitment to Hong Kong under its new government, not only as the best regional centre, but also as the focus for auctions in Asia.

The two regular Hong Kong auction series held during the year were both highly successful, the highlight being a remarkable single-owner sale in the spring, comprising of only nine lots of Ming and Qing imperial porcelain (described on pp. 34–35). On the same day was the auction of a group of Buddhist stone sculptures from the collection of the late J. T. Tai, a leading dealer in Chinese art in New York, which attracted great interest from a new generation of sculpture collectors in Taiwan.

Another private collection of ceramics, concentrating on celadon ware, was sold the previous autumn, when a Song dynasty vase in the shape of an ancient jade cong made HK$5,630,000 (£450,400; $731,900, *bottom right*).

In the field of jewellery Hong Kong has long been established as the world centre for auctions of jadeite, the translucent green stone whose shades of colour are the subject of the keenest Chinese connoisseurship. Hong Kong is now also a major centre for the sale of Western-style jewellery, alongside New York, Geneva and London.

During the season five paintings sales were held in Asia, including two in Hong Kong, of works by a wide range of twentieth-century Chinese artists discerningly selected by the new head of department, C. K. Cheung. In Singapore the second sale of South-East Asian paintings was held, with high prices being achieved for works of Indonesian interest. In Taiwan two sales of Chinese oil paintings were held in this well-established niche market, where the works of two Chinese artists who worked in Paris, Sanyu and Pan Yuliang, are particularly appreciated.

The market in Chinese stamps has been exceptionally active in the past two years and from the beginning of 1997 Sotheby's Asia entered into a joint

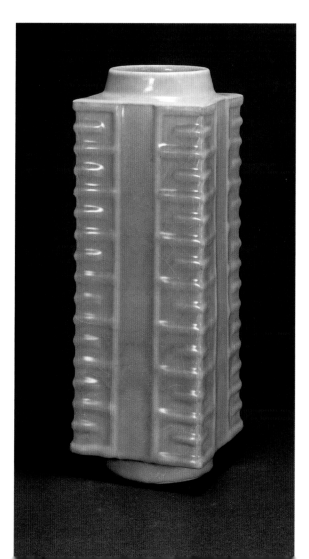

Poetic Landscape (above) by Zhang Daqian (1899–1983), painted in 1968, was auctioned in Sotheby's Hong Kong salerooms and reached a price of HK$4,640,000 (£371,200; $603,200).

A very large vase from the Longquan area (left), dating from the Southern Song Dynasty (1127–1279), this piece was one of the finest examples of celadons included in November's sale of a private collection.

venture with the Swiss stamp auctioneers, Corinphila, now led by the unrivalled team of Richard Ashton of Sotheby's and Geoffrey Schneider of Corinphila, both specialists in the Chinese issues. The turnover of the season's Hong Kong stamp auctions reached a remarkable HK$64,783,085 to which important contributions were made by the sales of the collections of the late M. C. Chow, and of the first two parts of the great collection of Chinese stamps belonging to Anna-Lisa and Sven-Eric Beckeman.

Sotheby's Japan has also had an active year under the dynamic leadership of Tetsuji Shibayama, with substantial rises in the amount of property sold in New York, London and Geneva for Japanese consignors, and purchases by Japanese buyers worldwide, signalling the long-awaited recovery in the Japanese art market, which has been depressed since the end of the 'bubble economy' seven years ago.

Buyers from Chinese Asia have also made an increasing impact on sales in New York, Geneva and London. Here the Client Services departments on both sides of the Atlantic have played an essential role, with Patricia Wong in London and Jean Kim in New York ensuring that all our Asian buyers receive the help they need in buying at auction.

AN ONGOING SECRET: THE PLEASURE OF OLD MASTER PAINTINGS

George Wachter

George Wachter is Executive Vice President and Managing Director, Fine Arts Division, Sotheby's New York.

My career at Sotheby's began in 1973, when, fresh out of college, where I had studied art history, I attended a Sotheby's Works of Art Course in London. Just as the course was ending, I was hired to join the Old Masters department as an expert. Of course, I was not an expert – the word was just a job title – and I quickly realized that I had been thrown into the deep end of a very deep pool. I soon found out that the Old Masters field, which covers European paintings from 1300 to 1800, encompasses a vast range of artists. For every Giotto, there is a Bartolomeo di Messer Bulgarini; for every Botticelli, a Michele di Ridolfo; for every Gainsborough, a William Owen.

Aware of my ignorance, which seemed to me to be of epic proportions, I nevertheless went bravely, if nervously, out to the counter every day to make my assessments. Fortunately, senior experts were always available to give help where needed, and Sotheby's London also had two great scholars working in the department: Philip Pouncey, a famous expert on Italian paintings and drawings, and Neil McLaren, who was equally famous for his knowledge of Dutch art.

Philip had a fascinating mind and was an excellent teacher. Some art historians have a photographic memory, and, once having seen something by an artist, they will instinctively recognize another work by the same artist, and will always remember each painting or photograph they've seen. Philip wasn't like that. He had to work his way methodically through every painting. He would come to a conclusion by finding clues based on his understanding of the artist's hand, personality or technique. If he did not remember seeing a painting, which in fact he had identified in the past, he would use the same method to come to his conclusion, and he would invariably come to the same conclusion he had reached years before. It was a fabulous education, but quite daunting because he would say, 'This is by Domenico de Angelis, a student of Marco Benefial,' and

you would not have heard of either one of them. Seeing your confusion, he'd look at you teasingly, then say, 'Well, every taxi driver in London has heard of these artists!'

Another valuable aspect of my Old Masters education was that in the 1970s paintings by towering figures such as Veronese, Rubens and Dirck Bouts were possible to find but becoming increasingly rare and prohibitively expensive. As a consequence, collectors turned to (then) lesser-known artists in their search for wonderful paintings. Subsequently, the prices for these artists began to climb as well, and collectors again broadened their interest, a natural cycle that continues up to the present day. There always seem to be good artists that can be discovered.

In my early career, I had some memorable experiences with an artist who perfectly illustrates this progression. I remember the shock when, in December 1975, a small but beautiful landscape by Jan Brueghel the Elder, which was illustrated in black and white and which we estimated at £20,000 to £30,000, was sold for £73,000. The market had woken up for this artist.

Two years later, in 1977, I was transferred to Sotheby's New York, and shortly thereafter I went to look at a painting by Dirck Hals in an apartment at the UN Plaza. As I was leaving, I noticed a flower picture almost hidden behind a door. Although the painting was under glass and was difficult to see, I thought, 'Either this is a Jan Brueghel or it's a photograph of one.' I politely asked the owner to deliver it to Sotheby's for an evaluation. When the glass was removed, we found a stunningly beautiful painting by Jan Brueghel the Elder in perfect condition. We estimated it at $100,000 to $120,000 and it sold for $560,000.

Then, a year later, I had an appointment at the counter to see a painting by Jan van Os, a good Dutch eighteenth-century flower painter. The man opened the package and out came another Jan Brueghel the Elder, this time on copper. (By then I was feeling pretty comfortable with this artist.) Research proved that the painting had been owned by Napoleon's brother, Joseph Bonaparte, who was living in Bordentown, New Jersey, in 1845. He had a sale of his paintings and the Jan Brueghel was catalogued as a Jan van Os at that early date, and it had remained a van Os until I recognized the artist's true identity that day at Sotheby's. The work sold for $410,000. This painting and the Jan Brueghel I found in the apartment at the UN Plaza can today both be seen at the Kunsthalle in Zurich.

Based on these two finds, and the innocence of youth, I thought perhaps I could expect to identify a Jan Brueghel the Elder every year! In today's market, a great Jan Brueghel the Elder, whether landscape or still life, would be valued at $2 to $3 million.

Like the market for my Brueghels, the Old Masters market has grown stronger. During the early 1990s Old Masters proved recession-proof, largely because the market is not supported by one group but relies on many different national economies. For example, the early 1990s were not great years to sell Dutch pictures,

Hung behind a door and obscured by a piece of glass, *Flowers in a Glass Vase* was discovered to be by Jan Brueghel the Elder and sold for $560,000 on 13 January 1978.

The Birth Salver of Lorenzo de' Medici. Recto: *The Triumph of Fame* by Lo Scheggia was commissioned by Piero de' Medici to commemorate the birth in 1449 of his first son, Lorenzo 'il Magnifico'. Originally in the collection of The New-York Historical Society, it can now be seen at the Metropolitan Museum of Art in New York.

but prices for Italian pictures, particularly those that appealed to the Italian market rather than the international market, were soaring.

At Sotheby's New York, in the fifteen years since I became the Director of the Old Masters Painting department, it's been my great privilege to preside over the sale of many of the outstanding Old Masters paintings collections to ever come to auction. A highlight of not only my career, but Sotheby's Old Masters sales in this century occurred on 12 January

1995, when Sotheby's New York auctioned 180 paintings from The New-York Historical Society, New York's oldest cultural institution, which regretfully was forced to sell its Old Masters collection. The interest was so high that people would not stop bidding. It was not unusual for a painting estimated at $10,000 to $15,000 to realize ten times that amount. The morning session of this sale went so late that Dede Brooks, Sotheby's President and CEO, ordered hundreds of sandwiches made, and lunch was served right in the auction room in order to expedite the beginning of the afternoon session!

It is gratifying that in 1997 the Old Masters sales have reached new heights. In January in New York, Sotheby's Old Masters sale realized the highest total ever made by an Old Masters sale: $47,690,850 (£29,568,327). Michael Sweerts' *Plague in an Ancient City* from the Saul P. Steinberg Collection sold for $3,852,500 (purchased by the Los Angeles County Museum, see p. 49), and Willem Drost's dashing *Portrait of an Officer in a Red Beret*, which was estimated at $150,000 to $200,000 sold for $2,697,500 (see p. 44).

In July, Sotheby's London sale of Old Masters set two world auction records for the artists Frans Hals (£1,926,500, see p. 50) and Gerard ter Borch (£2,751,500 , see p. 51) and saw five other lots selling above £1 million each.

When I began at Sotheby's London, the typical auction room was filled with dealers and a scattering of private collectors. One of the most dramatic changes has been that private collectors now actively compete with dealers, because people have discovered that they enjoy the auction process. They seem to like coming to the auction and being part of the excitement, and take comfort in the fact that there is usually someone else bidding on the work of art they want. They like having the estimate published, and they enjoy being able to get other people's opinions about their chosen paintings during the week the works are up for review.

What has not changed is that the Old Masters field attracts a very thoughtful person – whether a dealer or a collector – who likes to study and think about art. It has been my great pleasure to work with these collectors and dealers over the years, and to work with the paintings themselves, in all their infinite variety, complexity and beauty.

While it's thrilling to see a major Old Master artist break world auction records, it's also very satisfying to watch as a lesser-known painter starts to be recognized and collected. Presently hanging in my office is a beautiful painting in pristine condition by the sixteenth-century Mannerist, Michele di Ridolfo. A few years ago, this artist was selling in the $20,000 range, but this painting is a masterpiece and could now easily make $200,000. There continue to be fine Old Master painters who are still to be recognized. It is wonderful to see them come into their own. It is also gratifying when collectors who are originally attracted to other areas of painting realize what their money can buy if they begin collecting in Old Masters. I love welcoming them into the fold.

Annibale Carracci's *Boy Drinking* (above) was just one of the many important paintings that made up the brilliant collection of Old Master Paintings assembled by Peter Jay Sharp. This particular work was purchased by the Cleveland Museum of Art for $2,202,500 (£1,468,300) on 13 January 1994.

The work of Mannerist artist Michele di Ridolfo is currently being reassessed and his standing redefined. This example (left) – an allegorical figure that appears to be one of a group of female heads – sold in London on 11 December 1996 for £54,300 ($89,595), more than twice its pre-sale low estimate.

SOTHEBY'S ROLE IN THE HISTORY OF WESTERN MANUSCRIPTS

Christopher de Hamel

Dr Christopher de Hamel FSA is a Senior Director and Head of the Western Manuscripts department, Sotheby's Europe.

The Western Manuscripts sale on 17 June 1997 included a fifteenth-century manuscript Breviary which had been sold at Sotheby's twice before, on 7 March 1785 and on 11 January 1886. On the first occasion it realized £1. 5s., on the second £18, and on its third appearance at auction this year it sold for £36,700 ($59,821). Few other departments at Sotheby's can match the regularity with which illuminated manuscripts come back for re-sale punctually every hundred years or so. The *Concise Oxford Dictionary* gives the word 'Sotheby's' as an English noun, defined there as 'A sale-room in London for books, MSS., &c.'. Those of us who catalogue manuscripts like to remind our colleagues in the nouveau-riche departments such as Impressionists and Jewellery that their work is simply included in the '&c.' of the dictionary's definition. Medieval manuscripts have been part of the core business of Sotheby's since the very beginning. The fact that every manuscript is unique and that it is quite common for owners to write their names in books means that we can often identify the same manuscripts coming back on to the market from one generation of collectors to the next.

The Beck Sale of Illuminated Manuscripts on 16 June furnished some very good examples of manuscripts returning to Sotheby's. The sale comprised only thirty-four lots, but it represented one of the most refined and most consistently high-quality collections put together in the second half of the twentieth century. Many of the books were very well known and were familiar from earlier publications and Sotheby's catalogues of the past. Twenty of the thirty-four lots had been sold at Sotheby's before. There were, for example, two magnificent manuscripts bought from the Chester Beatty sale here at Sotheby's in 1969, including a portion of a spectacular Lower Saxon Psalter of about 1210 which had made £18,000 in 1969 and now re-sold for £1,871,500 ($3,069,260), a hundredfold increase in

under thirty years (see p. 24). Three manuscripts came from the Dyson Perrins sales at Sotheby's in 1958–60, including the massively rich thirteenth-century St-Blasien Psalter from the Black Forest (*right*). In the Dyson Perrins sale in 1960 it had realized £62,000. Such a sum would have bought almost any work of art in the world at that time, and was then the second highest price ever paid for a medieval manuscript. In the Beck sale this year the St-Blasien Psalter sold for £2,531,500 ($4,151,660), and has slipped (just) into third place, but is still in the first rank. It certainly holds its saleroom honour intact.

It can be fascinating to plot the history of individual books backwards into the past and to watch how prices have risen in relation to each other. Another early gothic Psalter from the Beck sale, once in the Abbey of Buxheim, was first sold at Sotheby's in 1912 for £175. It was sold again in 1932 for £74 (those were the Depression years), in 1952 for £1,350, in 1965 for £1,700 (a bargain, surely) and now in 1997 for £84,000 ($137,760).

Three Books of Hours in the Beck sale, to take further examples, had long Sotheby's associations. One manuscript was French, one Italian and one Dutch. The Popincourt Hours, made in Paris around 1450, was first sold at Sotheby's in 1902 for £235, a considerable sum then. It was re-sold in 1959 for £4,800. In 1997 it realized £89,500 ($146,780). The Blandford Hours represents Florentine Renaissance book illumination at its finest around 1470. It was first sold at Sotheby's in 1921 for £2,600, and a second time in 1958 when it was bought for £6,200. It was thus worth about ten times the value of the French Book of Hours early this century, fell to about two-and-a-half times by the late 1950s (Italian art had slipped in fashion), and returned triumphantly to ten times in 1997, at £881,500 ($1,445,660). The Dutch Book of Hours (see p. 135) made £50 at Sotheby's in 1889, £18,000 in 1970, and in 1997 the bidding opened at about £200,000 and went up and up, ten thousand a time, to a telephone bidder at £1,002,500 ($1,644,100). This is by far the most expensive Dutch manuscript ever sold at auction, infinitely exceeding the very pleasing £166,500 ($274,725) for another Dutch Book of Hours in December 1996.

Note that illuminated manuscripts were never cheap. Even £50 in the 1880s was a good sum of money. Such books have always been valuable, and they look expensive, shimmering with gold. In the Middle Ages themselves, manuscripts were treasured and highly valued, which was partly simply because of the labour involved in making them. One of the Beck books, a Breviary made in Genoa, includes two dated signatures of the scribe, which reveal that he completed 297 leaves of text between 20 September 1485 and 1 May 1486 – approximately two pages a day. Thus the labour in writing a book like this in the fifteenth century might represent six months' salary. Illumination was extra. Another book sold in 1997, a fifteenth-century French manuscript of the *Roman de la Rose*, included a note that the cost of painting the initials came to 10 sous and 12 deniers. Early owners of manuscripts treasured them carefully.

Several manuscripts from the Beck sale spent long periods of their lives in single collections. A fragment of a Netherlandish Book of Hours was brought to England by 1528 and it then remained in the same English family from one generation to another in direct line until 1912. It has now, in fact, gone back again to the Netherlands nearly 500 years later. A twelfth-century book made at Lambach Abbey in Upper Austria remained in the monastery there until the late 1920s when the monks themselves, facing terrible inflation and failed harvests, were obliged to sell books they had owned for almost 800 years. This particular volume came through Sotheby's in 1974 (£5,500), and in 1997 realized £133,500 ($218,940), triumphantly bought by the Oesterreichische Nationalbibliothek, and it thus returns to Austria forever. A tenth-century Visigothic document probably belonged to the Spanish Abbey of San Millán de la Cogolla for 900 years until the nineteenth century; it was last sold at Sotheby's in 1972 (£720), and in the Beck sale realized £34,500 ($56,580) to the Spanish national archives. It, too, now goes home.

One manuscript in the Beck Collection that had a long Sotheby's association was the great ninth-century Gospel Book probably made at Metz (see p. 25). It once belonged to the nunnery of Ste-Glossinde in Metz and had very probably entered that convent through the divorced and apparently adulterous Queen Theutberga

One of over 200 illustrations that appear in the St-Blasien Psalter. This shows the baptism of Christ, with St John the Baptist on the right, and, top centre, the hand of God reaching down.

The Last Supper from the early-thirteenth-century First Psalter of Mechtild of Braunschweig. Judas, whose name is written in red on the right, reaches out his hand to Christ.

who, after her divorce from King Lothaire II of Lorraine in 858, joined the community as abbess from 867. The book is in astonishingly fresh condition, and was probably hardly used by the nuns except as a symbolic or holy object on the High Altar, for swearing oaths and carrying in processions. It doubtless remained in Metz until the French Revolution. By the mid-nineteenth century it had come into the possession of the flamboyant rogue, Guglielmo Libri (1803–69), a former teacher of mathematics in Pisa who came to France in 1830, and in 1841 became secretary to the commission to catalogue the provincial libraries of France. Libri was also an enthusiastic private collector of manuscripts, a fast-talking swashbuckling entrepreneur, probably a thief and even a forger, and was constantly on the run from the authorities. At various times, Libri was forced to sell his collections. The Gospel Book was brought by him to Sotheby's in 1859. The sale catalogue asserted that the consignor was an 'Eminent Collector, who is obliged to leave London in consequence of ill health'. Libri wrote his own description of the book, describing it extravagantly as 'one of the finest manuscripts of the Gospels ever offered for sale . . . and in the highest state of preservation'. It was illustrated in the sale catalogue with a full-page engraved plate (one of the earliest illustrated Sotheby's catalogues, *right*), and the book sold for £90.

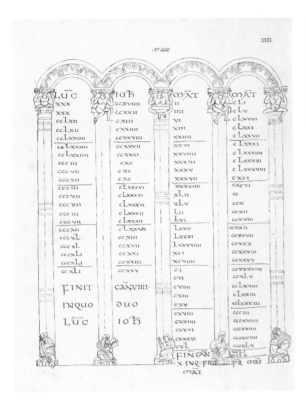

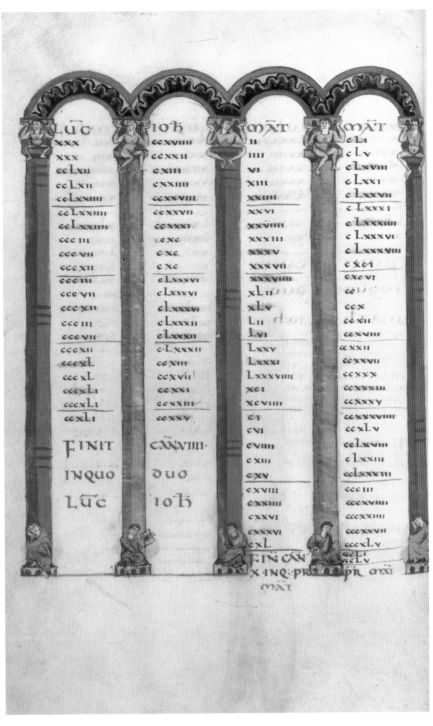

The next owners were quite different from Libri, and belonged to the infinitely respectable English professional classes. The buyer in 1850 was Sir William Tite (1798–1873), architect of many public buildings and great Victorian railway stations, and the principal designer of the Thames embankment. At his sale at Sotheby's in 1874 the Gospel Book sold for £89, a fall of £1 in fifteen years (those were the days of no inflation). It was bought by the Quaker banker Alexander, first Lord Peckover of Wisbech (1830–1919), a major collector of early Bibles. It was then reconsigned jointly by his two grandsons back at Sotheby's in 1933. This time it made £540, even in the Depression. It was bought that year by Charles Harry St John Hornby (1867–1946), partner in the bookselling firm of W. H. Smith and founder of the Ashendene Press. After his death it was sold (at a valuation of £2,000) to Major J. R. Abbey (1894–1969), sportsman and chairman of a great family brewing business, at whose sale at Sotheby's yet again in 1975 it now realized £80,000, to Bernard Breslauer for the Beck family. (The highest price then ever paid for any manuscript had recently risen to £90,000).

Now for the fifth time at Sotheby's, as lot 2 in the Beck sale on 16 June 1997, the Gospel Book sold for £1,101,500 ($1,806,460). We look forward to welcoming it back again in, say, 2020.

A folio from the Gospels of Queen Theutberga of Lorraine (above), c. 825–50. It was first sold through Sotheby's in 1859.

A page from the 1859 sale catalogue (above left), one of the first at Sotheby's to have illustrations, showing the Gospels of Queen Theutberga of Lorraine.

THE SHELBURNE MUSEUM COLLECTION

Alexander Apsis

Alexander Apsis is Head of the Impressionist and Modern Art department, Sotheby's New York.

The most notable event in the New York 1996–97 auction season in Impressionist and Modern Art was the sale of five works from the Shelburne Museum, Vermont. The Shelburne Museum was founded by Electra Havemeyer Webb in 1952 to foster a deeper understanding and appreciation of life in early- and mid-nineteenth-century New England. To establish a collection care endowment and acquisition fund for the museum, five works inherited by Electra Webb from her parents, Mr and Mrs H. O. Havemeyer, were sold by Sotheby's in New York on 12 November 1996.

The Havemeyers were among the earliest and certainly the greatest American collectors of French Impressionist art. If the collection of French Impressionists in the Metropolitan Museum in New York is second only to that of the Musée d'Orsay in Paris, it is because of the Havemeyer bequest of over 1,000 paintings and other works of art. Advised by Mary Cassatt, the Havemeyers began buying superb works by the Impressionists in 1875, primarily from the Impressionists' dealer and champion, Paul Durand-Ruel. Their collection of Degas in particular was the most complete ever assembled, and included over 120 works. Given the fact that the Havemeyers possessed impeccable taste, almost unlimited funds, excellent advisors and direct access to the best works of the Impressionists at an early stage, it is not surprising that the Havemeyer provenance is the most desirable among Impressionist collectors.

Two of the works in the 12 November sale were pastels by Edouard Manet, the finest to appear on the market in modern times. Manet took up the medium of pastel relatively late in his career. Although not as adventurous as Degas in this medium, pastel suited Manet's dazzling technique, eye for colour and sensitive elegance. The *Portrait de Mademoiselle Suzette Lemaire, de profil* ($2,917,500; £1,779,675, *top right*) depicts a charming Parisienne so beloved by Manet. The second pastel by Manet in the Shelburne group was the *Portrait de Constantin Guys* ($1,652,500; £1,008,025), an artist little known today. Manet's pastels tend to be much more fragile than those of Degas, and one of the most remarkable things about the two Shelburne works was their pristine condition.

The other three works were by Edgar Degas; two pastels and a bronze. All three are of ballet dancers, his most beloved subject (more than half the works of art produced by Degas are concerned with ballet). The bronze, *Petite danseuse de quatorze ans* ($11,882,500; £7,248,325, *far right*), is Degas' largest and most important sculpture, and is breathtakingly modern in its realism and simplification of form. To attach a real dress to a sculpture may not seem so unusual to a post-1960s audience, but at the time this was a truly revolutionary and disturbing concept. Today it is one of the icons of nineteenth-century sculpture, and its sale was a clear indication that the market for top-quality Impressionist and Modern works has now largely recovered from the slump of the early 1990s. The price achieved for this sculpture in November 1996 surpassed by over $1.5 million the previous record for a cast of the same bronze established in 1988, when the market is generally perceived to have been extremely strong. This was one of the many indications during the 1996–97 season that there is a large and growing number of collectors willing to bid strongly for the best quality Impressionist and Modern works.

The collector Charles Ephrussi was in the habit of obtaining commissions for portraits for his Impressionist friends by introducing them to his wide circle of fashionable acquaintances. He introduced flower painter Madeleine Lemaire to Manet and she requested this portrait of her daughter, Suzette.

Sotheby's New York headquarters announce the sale of the Shelburne Collection.

Petit danseuse de quatorze ans shocked the public with its realism. Critics likened the girl to a rat, and saw her as 'a precociously depraved flower'.

JOHN SINGER SARGENT'S *CASHMERE*

Peter Rathbone
and Dara Mitchell

Peter Rathbone and **Dara Mitchell** are both Senior Vice Presidents and Heads of the American Paintings, Drawings and Sculpture department, Sotheby's New York.

The American paintings and sculpture market exhibited remarkable strength in December 1996. Unlike many other collecting fields that are known for their sharp peaks and valleys, the American market has consistently achieved record prices, particularly for impressive works by top-tier nineteenth- and early-twentieth-century American artists. Sotheby's has had the privilege and opportunity to have sold the lion's share of the most distinguished American works offered at public auction. Of the top twenty prices achieved in New York for American paintings, Sotheby's has been responsible for fifteen.

The December 1996 American Paintings and Sculpture sale was a landmark event in several respects. The sale total of $34,193,725 (£20,858,172) was the third highest in the history of this specialized collecting field, exceeded only by sale totals of $37,258,925 (£20,699,402) in December of 1987 and $37,785,550 (£21,968,343) in May of 1989, both of which occurred at Sotheby's. The sale included many outstanding pieces by a variety of American artists, but it was John Singer Sargent's *Cashmere* that commanded the greatest attention from the moment it was announced that the painting would be sold at auction to the moment it went on the block. When it was finally hammered down at $11,112,500 (£6,778,625), applause and disbelief spread through the room, and a new auction record was set, eclipsing the previous record of $8,250,000 (£5,254,777) for Frederic Edwin Church's *Home by the Lake*, which sold at Sotheby's in 1989.

Cashmere is an extremely rare and important example of Sargent's work and has been acknowledged by scholars to be among the most mature and elaborate of the artist's late Alpine figural subjects. An ambitious composition that evokes the rhythmic elegance of a classical figural procession, *Cashmere* is an arresting image of beauty and exoticism. The model for the

painting was Reine Ormond, Sargent's niece, variously draped in a cashmere shawl and painted by Sargent in seven different poses in a frieze-like arrangement across the canvas. The aura of mystery that envelops the painting, and Sargent's unusual device of repeating the same stunning, cloaked model in multiple poses makes it a unique image in Sargent's oeuvre. Interestingly, Sargent painted *Cashmere* on two separate canvases during a sojourn in the Alps, which he then joined, probably back in his London studio, to create a single painting.

The complex figural arrangement and the size of the work reveals Sargent's conception of it as an exhibition piece intended for the Royal Academy of 1909. It was bought during this exhibition by one of Britain's most important collectors, Robert Henry Benson, and remained in his family's collection until it was sold at Sotheby's in 1996. One especially thrilling aspect of its appearance at Sotheby's in New York was the fact that the painting had never before been exhibited in the United States, and had not been publicly exhibited since 1979, when it was shown at the National Portrait Gallery in London, in *John Singer Sargent and the Edwardian Age*.

While we were incredibly fortunate to be given the opportunity to offer such a wonderful work of art, the fantastic price *Cashmere* achieved marked the culmination of a successful record with this artist. In May 1996, just six months before we sold *Cashmere*, *Capri Girl* (*Dans les oliviers, à Capri*) fetched $4,842,500 (£3,196,050) in the very same rooms, and of course there is the memorable *Spanish Dancer*, sold in 1994 for what then seemed like a staggering sum – $7,592,500 (£5,011,050). We look forward to offering great paintings for sale at Sotheby's in the future, both by Sargent and others, and feel that the American paintings market has broken through to a new plateau where expectations for the finest works have clearly increased.

Cashmere (above) was painted by Sargent in 1908. Most of his Alpine studies were exhibited at the New English Art Club, but he considered *Cashmere* important enough to be shown at the Royal Academy, where it appeared, to very appreciative reviews, in 1909.

Sargent (left) sketching in the Alps, about 1906–10. *Cashmere* was painted in 1908 in Purtud, an Alpine town on the Italian–Swiss border that Sargent visited frequently between 1904 and 1913.

FAUVE AND EXPRESSIONIST ART FROM THE COLLECTION OF CHARLES TABACHNICK

Melanie Clore and
Helena Newman

Sonnenuntergang (*Sunset*, 1909) by Emil Nolde reflects his belief that colour can be used to express moods and emotions. Nolde wrote, 'Every colour holds within it a soul, which makes me happy or repels me, and which acts as a stimulus.'

The best collections, besides bringing together works of outstanding merit, transcend their contents by offering insights both into the history of art and into the mind of the collector. The collection of paintings and sculpture formed in the 1960s and 70s by the Canadian Charles Tabachnick brought to light a fascinating and rarely explored subject: the affinity between the art of the French Fauves and the German Expressionists. A superb group of five paintings by the Fauve artist Kees Van Dongen dating from 1897–1910 was combined with rare works by German Expressionist artists such as Heinrich Campendonk, Alexej von Jawlensky, Ernst Ludwig Kirchner, Hermann Max Pechstein and Emil Nolde.

By juxtaposing works from the two artistic movements each artist could be appreciated in a broader international context. In the event, the success of the sale was a resounding vindication both of the concept that German Expressionist art should not be seen in a vacuum and of Sotheby's unique policy of

including the best examples of German twentieth-century art alongside those of the other major modern European masters. Sold in London on the same evening as the Part I Impressionist and Modern Art sale, in which a world record of £8.8 million ($14.7 million) was set for a work on paper by van Gogh (see pp. 74–75), the collection exceeded all expectations. Further world records were set for all the German Expressionist artists represented and for Van Dongen and a bronze by Henri Laurens.

One of the most important paintings in the collection was the oil by the *Brücke* artist Ernst Ludwig Kirchner *Strassenszene* (*Street Scene*) of 1913 (see p. 85). Directly relating to the monumental series of Berlin street scenes which are amongst Kirchner's most celebrated paintings, it is one of the few remaining oils of this subject still in a private collection. Kirchner first visited Berlin in 1910 and moved there from Dresden in 1911 to join the other artists of the *Brücke*. The dynamic metropolitan life of the city soon had a profound

Melanie Clore (top) is a Senior Director and Head of the Impressionist and Modern Art department, Sotheby's Europe.

Helena Newman (above) is a Senior Director in the Impressionist and Modern Art department, Sotheby's Europe, and specializes in German Expressionist Art.

influence on Kirchner's subject matter and style. The Berlin 'cocottes', with their elongated figures and mannequin-like appearance are rendered here with energetic hatching that was to become the hallmark of Kirchner's mature Expressionist style. The painting sold for £1,981,500 (estimate: £1,300,000–1,600,000).

The artists of the *Brücke*, which was founded in Dresden in 1905, did not develop in isolation from their colleagues in neighbouring countries: van Gogh was exhibited in Dresden in 1905, whilst Munch first showed in Berlin as early as 1892. In 1908 Pechstein travelled to Paris where he became acquainted with Van Dongen, whom he subsequently invited to join the *Brücke*. It was probably Van Dongen who in turn arranged for the Fauves to exhibit alongside the Brücke at the Galerie Emil Richter in Dresden in 1908. This association was reflected in the Tabachnick Collection. Van Dongen's monumental *Femme au grand chapeau* of 1906 fetched £2,201,500 (see p. 83, estimate: £1,000,000–1,500,000) and Pechstein's

Zwei Mädchen (*Two Girls*) of 1909 fetched £837,500 ($1,400,740, estimate £300,000–400,000). Emil Nolde, who was invited to join the *Brücke* in 1906, was represented by the dramatic and fiery landscape *Sonnenuntergang* (*Sunset*) of 1909 which made £1,046,500 ($1,750,290, estimate: £600,000–800,000, *opposite*). Paintings by artists associated with the *Blaue Reiter* movement complemented those by the *Brücke* artists so that the collection encompassed both these important strands of Expressionism. A striking still life by Jawlensky of 1905 fetched £1,211,500 (estimate: £250,000–350,000, see p. 84) and a rare Orphist-influenced painting by Heinrich Campendonk, *Der Balkon* (*The Balcony*) of 1913, realized £958,500 ($1,603,110, estimate: £250,000–350,000, *below*).

At the end of the sale, not only had a rare collecting intelligence been honoured, but one more step had been taken in restoring German Expressionism to its rightful place in the canon of modern art.

Der Balkon (*The Balcony*) by Heinrich Campendonk. The artist was strongly influenced by Franz Marc and Wassily Kandinsky and was invited by them to join the *Blaue Reiter* group in 1911.

AVANT-GARDE PHOTOGRAPHS OF THE 1920s AND 1930s: THE HÉLÈNE ANDERSON COLLECTION

Philippe Garner

Lotte by Max Burchartz was shot in the late 1920s, and sold in May 1997 for £67,500 ($109,350).

The sale of the Hélène Anderson Collection of Photographs in London on 2 May 1997 is sure to be remembered by all those present as a landmark event in the history of the market. The main saleroom was packed to capacity. Unusually in an art market in which absentee bidding, particularly on major lots, has become the norm, there was very little telephone activity, and the auctioneer's catalogue contained very few commission bids. The sheer quality and rarity of the material on offer and its fascinating background story had stimulated such a mix of excitement and curiosity that most major players in this field – dealers, collectors and curators – had decided to be present in London and to enjoy personal participation in this historic auction. Bidding battles were fought out in the room as numerous records were set for individual photographers and, after nearly four hours of intense competition through the 221 lots, a new

record was set for any collection of photographs ever offered at auction.

The story of the Hélène Anderson Collection is the stuff of an auctioneer's dream. A chance enquiry through Sotheby's Frankfurt office led to the revelation of a top-quality collection of stunning images illustrating the power of avant-garde photography of the 1920s and early 1930s. The prints, which included images by Florence Henri, Man Ray, Umbo and Edward Weston, were preserved for the most part in quite remarkable condition. They had not been seen since before World War II and surfaced as a complete surprise, fresh to the market-place and corresponding perfectly to the desires of collectors well aware of the importance and extreme rarity of such material.

Who was Hélène Anderson and through what circumstances was her name destined to be linked so emphatically to this distinguished group of photographs?

- Shells -

Edward Weston 1927
13/50

Shells (1927) by Edward Weston sold for £110,500 ($179,010), setting a new world record for the photographer.

Her son, who consigned the collection to Sotheby's for sale, explained that his mother had been born in Bunzlau in Silesia in 1891. Her family enjoyed sufficient means to support her move with her sister to Berlin to study art and, in Hélène's case, to pursue her interest in photography. She settled in Berlin and practised as a photographer, but it was not for this talent that her name has now entered the history of photography. It is rather for another, ultimately more important talent, that of recognizing qualities and merit in the work of other photographers. Her significant contribution to photographic history was in securing for posterity the precious prints that so well reflect the strength and lasting importance of the so-called New Vision in photography, which found such a forceful expression in Germany in the decade prior to the rise of the Nazis around 1933.

We can speculate, but have no hard evidence to show how the photographs were acquired by Anderson. It seems unlikely that she was an independent collector in the conventional sense, as the modern idea of collecting photographs was not a part of the culture of those times, there was no market-place for such work and she would not have been able to buy contemporary prints easily through galleries. Strands of circumstantial evidence and aspects of the photographs themselves suggest that it is likely that she was personally involved in avant-garde photographic circles, perhaps as part of a curatorial team working on promoting, collecting or exhibiting the most distinguished contemporary work. Evidently concerned to protect this cultural heritage from the risks of damage or loss in wartime Berlin, little could she have imagined, when she packed and sent the collection away for safekeeping in 1939, the dramatic events of 2 May 1997 that would celebrate its rediscovery.

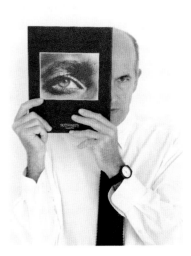

Philippe Garner is a Senior Director and Head of the Photograph and Applied Art departments, Sotheby's Europe.

MING AND QING PORCELAIN FROM A PRIVATE COLLECTION

Julian Thompson

Julian Thompson is Co-Chairman, Management Board, Sotheby's Asia.

Four pieces (opposite, top) from the April 1997 sale: far right and left, a pair of *famille-rose* 'peach' bowls; centre left, a rare 'lotus pond' jar; centre right, the 'yellow ground' landscape bowl.

This *famille-rose* 'peach' dish (right) was made between 1723 and 1735. The symbolic associations of the design are complex, and include connections with the spring, symbolized by the peach blossom, and with the wish for a long Imperial reign.

This 'dragon' washer (far right) has survived in remarkable condition for over 560 years.

The series of sales in Hong Kong in spring 1997 included a remarkable group of Ming and Qing Imperial porcelain from a distinguished Far Eastern collection formed with exceptional taste and discrimination in the late 1980s. Five of the nine lots offered fetched in excess of $1 million each, and prices exceeded levels reached at the peak of the market in 1989 when the auction of Chinese porcelain from the British Rail Pension Fund broke all previous records. In fact, new price records were set in two important areas, in Ming blue and white, and in Qing porcelain. The strongest bidder in the sale was Eskenazi Ltd, London, who obtained three of the five major lots, against strong competition from Far East buyers, particularly from Taiwan.

The porcelain was exhibited in a specially designed installation at the Furama Hotel, Hong Kong so that it could be seen in safety by the large numbers of people who were drawn to the weekend preview of the auctions.

Three of the major pieces in the sale dated from the golden years of Qing Imperial porcelain in the second quarter of the eighteenth century, when the *famille-rose* palette reached a high point of perfection. The first lot in the sale was the large 'peach' dish (*right*) which fetched HK$15,200,000 (£1,216,000; $1,976,000). Its decoration is highly auspicious as peaches are emblematic of longevity, and the five bats that fly among the branches represent the five happinesses of human life – old age, wealth, health, love of virtue and a natural death. The dish was originally sold at Sotheby's New York in 1989 from the Van Slyke Collection. With the same decoration and also bearing the reign mark of

the Yongzheng emperor, the dish was followed by the pair of bowls (*top, far right and left*) at HK$9,040,000 (£723,200; $1,175,200). These also had distinguished provenance, coming from the renowned collection formed by the Boston collector Paul Bernat.

The highest price was, however, paid for the early Qianlong bowl (*top, second from right*), enamelled in Beijing for the emperor's personal use. Also from the Bernat Collection, it had fetched HK$7,920,000 (£561,702; $1,014,085) at Sotheby's Hong Kong in 1988 and now made HK$21,470,000 (£1,717,600; $2,791,100). The striking decoration of landscapes in puce monochrome on a lemon-yellow ground is elsewhere unrecorded, and it ranks among the masterpieces of Qing ceramics.

The two Ming pieces, both painted in underglaze-blue, date from the fifteenth century, when this style of decoration dominated the wares made for the palace. The 'dragon' washer (*far right*) is thinly made with the walls of the vessel following the outline of a ten-petalled flower. It bears the mark of the Xuande emperor (1426–35) and, unlike most pieces of this shape, which were extensively used and often damaged, it was in pristine condition, a major factor contributing to its price of HK$13,770,000 (£1,101,600; $1,790,100).

The last lot in the sale was the blue and white jar from the reign of Chenghua (*top, centre left*), freely painted with lotus and other water plants rising from breaking waves encircling the base, in the soft tone of blue covered with a waxy glaze so characteristic of the supremely refined imperial wares of the period. Despite a small chip on the rim it ended the sale triumphantly at HK$1,780,000 (£142,400; $231,400).

TUREEN BY THOMAS GERMAIN

Kevin Tierney
and Ian Irving

Kevin Tierney and **Ian Irving** are both Senior Vice Presidents and Heads of the Silver department, Sotheby's New York.

An unexpected attraction joined the Manets and Degas during the Impressionist Week at Sotheby's New York in November 1996, when people queued to see an extraordinary group of eighteenth-century French silver. Gleaming softly against the blue cloth walls stood rows of candelabra, wine coolers and platters from services once belonging to three crowned heads of Europe. In the centre of the room glowed the tureen, cover and stand, made by Thomas Germain (1673–1748) in Paris in 1733–34.

The reputations of the greatest French silversmiths are based partly upon legend since so much of their work perished in melts ordered by kings of France in 1689, 1708 and 1759 to finance the War of the League of Augsburg, the War of the Spanish Succession and the Seven Years' War. The Revolution continued the destruction. Little of the work of Thomas Germain and his workshop remains. In his case, nature itself played a part: the Lisbon earthquake of 1755 destroyed the service he made for King João V (reigned 1705–53).

The tureen is breathtaking at first sight and exquisite on close inspection; the silver ripples and flows with infinite variations of reflective polished and matte-chased surfaces, revealing Germain's mastery of the metal. The harmony and balance testify to an architect's eye, and the modelling of the boars, vegetables and game shows a sculptor's hand. Such talent earned him the title of '*sculpteur-orfèvre du roi*' in 1723, with the privilege of quarters in the galleries of the Louvre.

The tureen bears the arms of Louis-Philippe as Duc d'Orléans (1773–1850, King of the French 1830–48) and belongs, with its partner in the Firestone Collection at the Detroit Museum of Art, to the Penthièvre-Orléans Service. This is a term given to a large amount of silver of different makers and dates inherited by Louis-Philippe from his mother, the daughter of the Duc de Penthièvre (1723–93).

The silver was long thought to have been ordered by forebears of the Duc, but recent research by Christiane Perrin, Stéphane Boiron and Sotheby's suggests another possibility. The name Janssen appears in the 1765 inventory of François-Thomas Germain's workshop, associated with copper and pewter models for tureens with boar's-head handles, listed as '*pour M. de Janssin* [sic]'. Comparison of the swans and reeds in the coat of arms of the Janssen family with the same repeated motifs chased on the tureen stand adds heraldic significance to something previously viewed as pure decoration. Janssen (also spelt Janssin and Jansin) is believed to be Henry Janssen, a card-sharp who gambled at White's Club in London and subsequently fleeced visiting English aristocrats in Paris.

The next clue to ownership appears in an 1803 biography of the Duc de Penthièvre by Elizabeth Guénard, which relates that Janssen had been ordered to melt his silver to help finance the war, but instead arranged to sell it to the Duc's brother, the Comte d'Eu, in exchange for an annuity, the Comte having already surrendered a sufficient quantity of his own silver. Support for this story comes from traces of an engraved coat of arms on the liner of the tureen, which, though now covered, can, with the help of an x-ray, be read as the royal arms of France as borne by a Prince of the Blood. The service passed from the Comte d'Eu to his brother, the Duc de Penthièvre, and, though seized during the Revolution, was spared as being of special quality, '*precieux par son execution*'.

The tureen descended in the family of Louis-Philippe until purchased by Mrs Ortiz Linares in 1952, and was inherited by her son George in 1980. The gasps of wonder at the exhibition were echoed by those in the saleroom as the bidding exceeded $9 million; the final price was $10,287,500 (£6,275,375), three times the previous auction record for a work in silver.

This Louis XV Royal silver tureen (right and bottom) with cover, liner and stand is an exquisitely detailed example of Thomas Germain's work.

The Royal French silver (below) was the property of George Ortiz, which he inherited from his mother, the collector Doña Graziella Patiño de Ortiz Linares.

THE ANDREW LLOYD WEBBER WINE COLLECTION

Serena Sutcliffe

Serena Sutcliffe MW is a Senior Director and Head of Sotheby's International Wine department.

London in May 1997 saw the sale of the greatest wine cellar ever to be auctioned. It was also the most important single-owner sale of wine, and therefore broke all records at a stroke or – should one say – at a gulp. The sale raised an outstanding total of £3,692,821 ($6,056,783) against a pre-sale high estimate of £2.7 million ($4.4 million).

Lord Lloyd Webber amassed a remarkable cellar of predominantly French wines before realizing that he had enough bottles to last many lifetimes. His decision to sell 18,000 of these bottles came at a time when the market was thirsty for fine wine, a situation that shows signs of continuing. Traditional markets for fine wines have been joined by countries that are newer to wine collecting; Asia is very active and Latin America is coming on to the scene. The market for fine wine is now truly global, with demand running ahead of supply, especially at the top end of the quality ladder.

The Andrew Lloyd Webber Wine Collection was rich in superb Bordeaux, the most desirable wines at auction. It also included a great array of white and red Burgundies from the best domains, as well as prestigious Champagnes and fine Rhône wines. Vintages ranged from the historic year of 1900, to 1993 red Burgundies, a classic year for ageing further.

The auction was spread over three sessions, starting with a gala evening sale. More than 12,000 bids were received, and the full room competed with commission and telephone bidders defying time zones. The combination of superb wine, great provenance, a looming millennium and the appearance on the market of the expensive 1996 Bordeaux futures proved catalytic. The sale provided a unique opportunity to acquire some of France's most desirable wines in perfect condition and in significant quantities.

One of the many highlights of the collection was the Millennium Dream Cellar Super Lot which sold for £242,000 ($396,880), establishing a new auction record for a single lot of wine sold at Sotheby's. Comprising one imperial, three double-magnums, two jeroboams, seventy-seven magnums and 265 bottles of historic wines ranging from Margaux 1900 to Corton Renardes 1990 from Leroy, this stellar capsule cellar was bought by Barrie Larvin, Master Sommelier and Director of Wines at the Rio Hotel Group in Las Vegas, Nevada.

Another dazzling lot which attracted considerable attention was the Bordeaux First Growth Super Lot, which could be described as a hedonist's paradise. It comprised all the First Growths in vintages in which they surpassed even themselves and included sixty bottles each of Lafite 1986, Latour 1990, Margaux 1990, Mouton Rothschild 1982, Haut Brion 1989 and Cheval Blanc 1982. It sold for £121,000 ($198,440), well above its high estimate of £85,000 ($139,400).

Wines from the landmark 1947 vintage, celebrating its fiftieth anniversary this year, were among the most coveted of the entire cellar. Three cases of the sensational Château Latour à Pomerol 1947, with its pure enticing fruit, each sold for an outstanding £35,200 ($57,728) – an unprecedented price for this vintage. The sweet, thick-textured and roasted fruit-laden Château Cheval Blanc 1947 was another high-flyer – a case also sold for £35,200 ($57,728) – and the same price was paid for six magnums of Château Pétrus 1947.

This was a landmark sale for wine at a time when interest has never been higher.

One of a pair of magnums of Romanée-Conti 1971. The lot sold for £5,500 ($9,020).

Lord Lloyd Webber started collecting wine when he was still at school, and describes himself as an 'incurable collector'. He decided to sell part of his collection when a stocktaking exercise made him realize the astonishing number of bottles he had amassed.

FINE ARTS

Lucas Cranach the Elder
The Judgement of Paris
Signed with the artist's
device of a winged dragon
Oil on limewood panel,
43 × 32.2 cm (17 × 12¾ in)
London £1,981,500
($3,269,475) 11.XII.96

In an unusual treatment of
a classical subject, Cranach
follows closely the text of a
medieval romance by Guido
da Columna, the *Historia
destructionis Troiae*. This
version of the legend has
Paris losing his way in a
thicket and falling asleep.
This latently erotic version
has the three goddesses
Venus, Juno and Athena,
whose beauty Paris must
judge, appearing in a dream
with an unfamiliar armour-
clad and aged Mercury.
Presenting Paris as a knight
in armour entranced by the
vision before him, Cranach
counterpoints the arts of love
against the art of war. From
as early as the sixteenth
century, the forest was seen
in German art as a source of
spiritual and cultural
renewal, often giving rise to
fantastic events. The sylvan
setting here is thus the
natural backdrop for the
relation of the myth.

English School

The Crucifixion

c. 1395

Tempera and oil-based paint
with gilded tin-relief, part
gold-ground on baltic oak
panel, 92.5 × 48.5 cm
(36½ × 19 in)
London £1,541,500
($2,589,720) 3.VII.97

The attribution of early panel
paintings to the English
School is problematic given
the paucity of art of this
nature surviving the
Reformation with which to
make comparison.
Nevertheless, the
iconographic and typological
similarities between this
picture and English
monumental painting of the
end of the fourteenth century
make a very compelling case
for it being a rare survivor
from this once-flourishing
school. The fact that many of
the artists working in England
at the time were immigrants,
bringing with them
influences of their local
school, makes the definition
of specifically English
characteristics more
complicated. Certain
features, however, such as
the distinctive background of
gilt tin-relief, whilst occuring
in other parts of Europe early
in the century, seem to have
been used solely in England
by the time this panel was
painted; similar techniques
can be found, for example, in
the Thornham Parva retable
in East Anglia.

Willem Drost
Portrait of an Officer in a Red Beret
1654
Oil on canvas, 102.9 × 92.1 cm (40½ × 36¼ in)
New York $2,697,500 (£1,672,450) 30.1.97

Willem Drost's oeuvre includes biblical subjects, portraits and allegorical figures. All his dated works are from the period 1652–63 during which time, it has been suggested, he trained under Rembrandt. His early works clearly show the older painter's influence, although there is no record of his apprenticeship, and not even the dates of his birth and death are known. The high quality of his work has led some scholars to consider attributing to him works formerly thought to be by Rembrandt or his anonymous followers. *Portrait of an Officer in a Red Beret* is signed and dated *Drost pinxit 1654*.

Rembrandt Harmensz. van Rijn

Bust-length Portrait of an Old Man with a Beard
Signed and dated
Rembrandt .1633
Oil on paper mounted on panel, 10.8 × 7 cm (4¼ × 2¾ in)
New York $2,972,500
(£1,842,950) 30.1.97
From the Collection of Saul P. Steinberg

There has been speculation on the original function of this work – Rembrandt's smallest painting – since it is small, monochrome and on an unusual support – paper. It may have been a study in preparation for a print, or it could have been an *aide-memoire* or souvenir of a close friendship, or a gift to a good friend, which would explain the prominence of the date and signature. It will be on loan to the National Gallery of Victoria, Melbourne, Australia between October 1997 and February 1998 for the exhibition, *Rembrandt: a Genius and his Impact*.

Giovanni Antonio Canale, called Canaletto

The Riva degli Schiavoni Looking East and *The Molo Looking West with the Column of Saint Theodore on the Right, Venice: A Pair of Paintings*
c. mid-1730s
Both oil on canvas, each: 46.4 × 76.8 cm (18¼ × 30¼ in)
New York $4,512,500 (£2,797,750) 30.1.97
From the Collection formed by the British Rail Pension Fund

Canaletto began his career as a theatrical designer under his father before working with landscapist and engraver Luca Carlevarijs, who had a great influence on his style and choice of subject matter. Like Canaletto, Carlevarijs painted the views of Venice with their crowds and gondolas, but Canaletto imbued them with a poetic quality, and was especially responsive to light and atmosphere. He was particularly popular with the British, who visited Venice as part of the Grand Tour, and the patronage of Consul Smith in Venice meant that a number of his paintings went to British owners. The dating of these two paintings is suggested by the deep, rich tonality, which is similar to four other definitively dated paintings of the mid-1730s. The views depicted are among the most famous – and most frequently painted – in Venice.

Tiziano Vecellio, called Titian

Portrait of a Venetian Admiral Dressed in Armour and Draped With a Red Cloak
Oil on canvas, 87 × 73.3 cm
(34¼ × 28¾ in)
London £1,211,500
($2,035,320) 3.VII.97

This is a late work by Titian and is particularly close in style to the artist's mythological works of the 1570s, considered by many to be his greatest and most expressive pictures. Late portraits by the artist are very rare and none are known after 1570. Employing the bold, free handling that is so characteristic of the artist at this period, Titian – by the time this picture was painted already into his eighties – portrays with great psychological insight the physical presence of a hoary naval commander who stares out at the viewer with a hawk-like gaze. A pen and ink drawing made after the painting by Sir Anthony van Dyck during his trip to Italy (1621–27) appears on the same page of his sketchbook as his copy of a portrait by Raphael which was in the Uffizi, Florence by 1589. This gives more clues to the precise whereabouts of this picture in the seventeenth century; however, the identity of the sitter still remains a mystery.

Joachim Antonisz. Wtewael
Diana and Actaeon
Signed and dated *joachim./
wten.wael fecit/1608*
Oil on copper, 15.9 × 21.3 cm
(6¼ × 8⅜ in)
New York $2,587,500
(£1,604,250) 30.1.97

Wtewael took his subject
from Book III of Ovid's
Metamorphoses. Actaeon,
who had spent the day
hunting, came across the
chaste goddess Diana
bathing in a stream. As a
punishment for seeing her
naked, Diana (who can be
identified by the crescent
moon near her head)
caused him to turn into a
stag by splashing him
with water. In this painting
the transformation has
begun, and Actaeon's dogs
eye him warily. When his
metamorphosis is complete
they will turn on him and
devour him. The painting's
whereabouts had not been
known for some time, but its
existence was confirmed by
a photograph published in
1929. The subject was treated
often by the artist, but this is
one of the most refined and
brilliant paintings in all of
Wtewael's oeuvre.

Michael Sweerts
Plague in an Ancient City
c. 1650
Oil on canvas, 118.7 ×
170.8 cm (46¾ × 67¼ in)
New York $3,852,500
(£2,388,550) 30.1.97
From the Collection of Saul
P. Steinberg

This painting, long attributed to Poussin, is quite unlike other paintings by Sweerts. For this reason, it is thought to have been a commission, and it has been suggested that the unknown patron suggested specific textual and pictorial sources to inspire the artist. The painting's most obvious

visual source is Poussin's *The Plague at Ashdod*, now in the Louvre in Paris. Sweerts may also have drawn upon a description of a plague sent by Juno to the island of Aegina in Book VII of Ovid's *Metamorphoses*, the victims of which 'flee from their own homes: for each man's home seems a place of death to

him' and are seen 'wandering half dead along the ways while they could keep on their feet. Others lying on the ground and weeping bitterly, turning their dull eyes upward with a last weak effort, and stretching out their arms to the sky that hung over them like a pall'.

Frans Hals
Saint John the Evangelist
Oil on canvas, 69.5 × 55 cm
(27.5 × 22 in)
London £1,926,500
($3,236,520) 3.VII.97

This portrait of Saint John is
the long-lost fourth painting
of a set depicting each of the
Evangelists. They were
known as a group from 1760
when they appeared at an
auction in The Hague.
Acquired for Catherine the
Great, the set remained in
the Hermitage until 1812,
when they were sent, with
thirty other paintings, to the
Crimea to decorate local
churches. At this time they
appear to have become
separated. Comparison of
the composition of this
portrait with that of the
others of Saints Matthew,
Mark and Luke (all lit from
the left and all depicted with
their customary attributes
beside them), clearly shows
that this is indeed the
missing Evangelist.

Gerard ter Borch

The Music Lesson
Oil on canvas, 66 × 53.5 cm
(26 × 21 in)
London £2,751,500
($4,622,520) 3.VII.97

This is the best rendition of a popular composition known in several versions and numerous copies, some of which have been confused in the past. The young woman plays a theorbo-lute with her teacher leaning solicitously over her shoulder. Given the age-old association between music and love, genre pictures such as this are generally thought to allude to love, often with a mercenary undertone. Although the bed in the background might suggest such a reading, there are no other hints in this particular picture to support any intention of salaciousness.

Raffaello Santi, called Raphael

Studies of the Christ Child
Numbered in pen and brown ink *J.95*
Red chalk, 22 × 16.7 cm
(8⅝ × 6½ in)
New York $310,500
(£192,510) 29.1.97

The Christ Child's pose in a Raphael workshop painting entitled *Holy Family with St John the Baptist* is based on these studies. The three drawings on this sheet all show Raphael working to define a pose for the child and studying the distribution of his weight. The figures are at an angle to the horizontal, since the child in the painting leans outwards, supported against the lap of his mother who kneels on the ground. A work of considerable importance and beauty, this drawing sheds significant light on Raphael's working methods.

Jacques Le Moyne de Morgues

Clove Pinks and a Small Tortoiseshell Butterfly
c. 1585, inscribed on verso 30
Gouache and gold leaf on vellum, 14.6 × 11 cm
(5¾ × 4⅜ in)
New York $140,000
(£86,800) 29.1.97
Property of the late Mr Eric Korner

In this exquisite gouache Le Moyne has created a highly sophisticated *trompe-l'oeil* effect, playing the delicately painted shadows off against the decorative borders, to give the illusion that the viewer is looking at actual plant specimens, enclosed in display boxes. Both in technique and overall visual richness the gouache is reminiscent of medieval manuscript illuminations.

Paulus Pontius and Sir Peter Paul Rubens

The Assumption of the Virgin
Numbered 14 and inscribed in brown ink
Black chalk, touches of pen and brown ink, with brown and grey wash, heightened with white and grey bodycolour and oil, 65.4 × 42.7 cm (25⅞ × 16⅞ in)
London £441,500 ($732,890)
2.VII.97
From the Collections of the Earls of Warwick

In 1624 Rubens published an engraving after his 1618 painting of the Assumption of the Virgin in the Church of Notre Dame de la Chapelle, Brussels. This drawing is the preparatory *modello* for the engraving, which was executed by Paulus Pontius, a member of Rubens' studio. Rubens himself transformed the careful black chalk copy of the altarpiece made by Pontius by reworking large areas to give slight but significant changes in the attitudes of many figures, adding an arched top with the figure of Christ receiving the Virgin and providing modelling and texture through a rich combination of penwork, bodycolour and oil. Though this drawing, which is one of the most extensively reworked designs for prints by Rubens that is known, was widely celebrated in nineteenth-century literature as a major work by Rubens, it had disappeared from view in this century until rediscovered by Sotheby's experts in the course of a valuation.

Circle of Robert Peake

Portrait of Three Young Girls
Oil on panel, 85 × 117 cm
(33½ × 46 in)
London £254,500 ($419,925)
13.XI.96

Only the Lothian, Glasfurd and Walton families bear a red hunting horn in their family crests, and it has been suggested that the sitters for this portrait are members of one of these families, as each wears a coral hunting-horn earring. The *punto in aria* lace worn by the girls was highly prized at the time, and could cost more than fine jewellery. The marigolds in the hair of the two youngest children are meant to ward away evil, and the semi-ripened fruit held by the two eldest is a sign of their immaturity and a suggestion of development in the future.

Alexander Cozens
After Rain
1760–75
Oil on paper, 23.5 × 30.5 cm
(9¼ × 12 in)
London £430,500 ($701,715)
9.IV.97
The Property of the Earl of
Warwick

This recently discovered oil
was painted in connection
with Cozens' planned series
of etchings entitled *The
Various Species of Composition
of Landscape in Nature*.
Cozens planned fifty-seven
etchings for the project
under three headings,
'Composition', 'Objects' and
'Circumstance', but only
made sixteen. This
particular oil came under

'Circumstance', intended to
be a series of twenty-seven
showing how accidents of
nature, such as storm and
fire, contribute to the
atmosphere and appearance
of landscape. Records
show that Cozens' son sold
ninety of his father's oils in
1794, but only eleven,
including this one, are
known to have survived.

Antonio Joli
The Thames looking towards Westminster and *The Thames looking towards the City*
1746
Oil on canvas, 109 × 173 cm (43 × 68 in) each
London £969,500 & £826,500 ($1,638,455 & $1,396,785) 9.VII.97
Property of the NatWest Group, sold for the benefit of the Lothbury Gallery

Joli arrived in London in 1744, following periods spent in Modena, Rome and Venice. The artist's stay in London gave him a clear understanding of English preferences in art, and ensured him extensive patronage from British Grand Tourists after his return to Italy in 1754. These spectacular panoramas of London capture the city at the height of its eighteenth-century prosperity and architectural beauty. Both include a formidable amount of topographical detail, highlighting the additions to the city following the Great Fire of 1666, such as the new Westminster Bridge and Christopher Wren's St Paul's Cathedral. The shore beneath the Cathedral is lined with new warehouses, the river is busy with a variety of boats and the Union Jack is prominent against the sky: all emphasize the city's increasing power and optimism.

John Frederick Herring, Snr
The Start for the Derby (1834)
Signed and dated *1834*
Oil on canvas, 101.6 ×
152.4 cm (40 × 60 in)
New York $1,487,500
(£922,250) 11.IV.97

One of the most celebrated painters of his age, and a favourite of British royalty, Herring was appointed the official animal painter to Queen Victoria's mother in 1845. William IV requested a private viewing on hearing of the scale and importance of this particular Derby composition. During his illustrious career Herring painted twenty-one Derby winners, thirty-four St Leger champions and eleven Oaks winners. A Herring portrait was considered by the winners to be the crowning glory to their success. His prowess as a horse painter can be seen to great effect in this picture, with the horses painted from all conceivable angles and at varying distances as they mill around at the start. Herring's figures and portraiture, the Achilles heel of many sporting artists, are also expertly drawn.

Richard Parkes Bonington
The Grand Canal, Venice, the Rialto in the Distance
Watercolour over pencil heightened with bodycolour and gum arabic, 18 × 28 cm (7 × 11 in)
London £84,000 ($136,080)
10.IV.97

Previously attributed to Thomas Shotter Boys, this watercolour is both an important rediscovery and a rare Venetian view by Bonington. The artist visited Venice in April and May 1826 with a patron, Charles Rivet. Inspired by the city, Bonington painted a number of pencil and watercolour sketches and some oils, all of which he could later use to produce finished works in his studio. Patrick Noon has suggested that this watercolour was painted in 1827, the year Bonington died. Characteristics of works dating from this time include an increased use of bodycolour in the architecture and staffage; this is particularly evident here in Bonington's depiction of the sky.

Joseph Mallord William Turner, RA
Hastings: Fish Market on the Sands, Early Morning
Signed and dated *1824*
Watercolour over pencil heightened with bodycolour and scratching out on wove paper, 44.5 × 66 cm
(17½ × 26 in)
London £199,500 ($323,190)
10.IV.97

This large watercolour, looking west towards Hastings, was one of a series commissioned from Turner by W. B. Cooke, whose intention was to engrave the series, but the intention was never carried out. The central group of figures is framed by others in Greek costume, referring to the Greek War of Independence, which was a

cause célèbre in Britain at the time. Eric Shanes suggests in *Turner's England* that the artist chose this view, close to the site of the last invasion of Britain in 1066, to make a statement about liberty and the loss of independence.

Albert Joseph Moore
*A Quartet: A Painter's Tribute
to the Art of Music,* AD 1868
Signed with anthemion
Oil on canvas, 61 × 88.3 cm
(24 × 34¾ in)
New York $662,500
(£410,750) 23.V.97

Albert Moore's *A Quartet*
is one of the supreme
achievements of English
aestheticism. The
philosophy of this
movement was that art
should address the spectator
in terms of mood and
emotion, without the
distraction of a narrative.
Here, no clues are given to

the relationship between
the figures or to their
personalities; rather, the
harmonies of colour, the
abstract rhythms of shape
and the arrangement of the
figures – almost like a
musical notation – convey
Moore's quest for
connections between the
arts of painting and music.

John Frederick Lewis

In the Bezestein, El Khan Khalil, Cairo
(The Carpet Seller)
Signed and dated *J. F. Lewis ARA/1860*
Oil on panel, 66 × 53.5 cm
(26 × 21 in)
London £551,500 ($921,005)
20.XI.96

During his residence in Cairo, from 1841 to 1851, Lewis made many sketches which provided the basis for oil paintings such as this, executed on his return to England. He was particularly attracted to the colours and patterns of the architecture, the jumble of merchandise and traders and the contrasts of light and shadow to be found in the bazaar. The Khan was once the centre of commercial traffic in Cairo, and Lewis' painting depicts a wealthy Turkish carpet trader enjoying a period of relaxation, while trade continues behind him. The degree of minute detail – from the orange peel on the table to the lattice work of the windows – was a talent for which Lewis was greatly admired by John Ruskin and the Pre-Raphaelites.

William Scott, RA
Still Life
Signed and dated 51
Oil on canvas, 115 × 153 cm
(45¼ × 60¼ in)
London £117,000 ($191,880)
18.VI.97

William Scott trained at the Belfast College of Art and the Academy Schools, London. He lived in France from 1937 to 1939, where he was influenced by the works of Cézanne and Bonnard. From the 1940s he concentrated on still-life subjects, particularly groups of kitchen objects, and described his interest in 'the still-life tradition of Chardin and Braque, leading to a certain kind of abstraction which comes directly from that tradition'. His work from the early 1950s became increasingly abstract.

Vanessa Bell
The Model
Signed and dated '13
Oil on canvas, 68.5 × 56 cm
(27 × 22 in)
London £95,000 ($154,850)
18.VI.97

Vanessa Bell was one of the
most cosmopolitan artists of
her generation and, as a
close associate of Roger Fry,
was well informed about the
work of post-Impressionist
artists such as Matisse and
Picasso. This portrait is
indicative of the degree to
which Bell had absorbed the
work of other artists, while
using a style that was
distinctly her own. The
background shapes show her
interest in pure abstraction
and the decorative arts, while
the flat planes of colour
modelling the face reveal the
influence of Matisse's
Woman with the Hat, 1905.

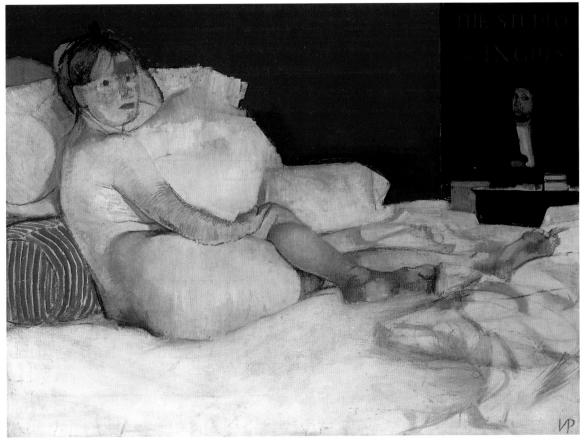

Victor Pasmore, CH, RA
The Studio of Ingres
1947, signed
Oil on canvas, 76.5 ×
101.5 cm (30 × 40 in)
London £221,500 ($361,045)
18.VI.97

The Studio of Ingres is
perhaps the defining image
of the movement that revived
British figurative painting in
the twentieth century. It also
shows Pasmore at a turning
point in his career as he
moved towards abstraction.
The position of the nude –
modelled by Pasmore's wife,
the painter Wendy Blood –
and the presence of the
bolster refer to harem
paintings by Ingres, and the
book cover on the right
anticipates pop art in its
ambiguous relationship with
the picture plane.

Sir Alfred James Munnings, PRA

H.M. The Queen's Horse 'Aureole' with the Queen's Trainer Captain Cecil Boyd-Rochfort, and Sir Humphrey Trafford at the 1953 Derby
1953, signed
Oil on cradled panel, unframed 55.2 × 75.6 cm (21¾ × 29¾ in)
New York $475,500 (£294,810) 11.IV.97

Formerly from the Estate of Ambassador Raymond R. Guest, Powhatan Plantation, King George, Virginia

'Aureole', a somewhat temperamental colt belonging to Queen Elizabeth II, came in second in the 1953 Derby, in the same week in which Edmund Hillary conquered Everest and the Queen was crowned at Westminster Abbey. Munnings had enjoyed the patronage of the British Royal family from the 1920s, and had previously been commissioned to paint many equestrian subjects. Another version of this subject is in the Queen's collection, portraying Her Majesty in discussion with Captain Boyd-Rochfort.

Jacques-Louis David
*Portrait of Suzanne Le Peletier
de Saint-Fargeau*
Signed and dated
L. David 1804
Oil on canvas, 60.5 × 49.5 cm
(23¾ × 19½ in)
London £3,741,500
($6,136,060) 11.VI.97
The property of the family of
the sitter

In 1804 David was appointed
First Painter to the Emperor
Napoleon, making him the
most influential artist of his
time. This portrait,
commissioned by the sitter
as a gift for her cousin and
future second husband, is
one of only a few that David
completed during the years
of the Empire. Suzanne was
the daughter of Louis-Michel
Le Peletier, a rich and liberal
revolutionary who was
proclaimed a 'martyr of
freedom' following his
assassination by a royalist.
Upon his death, Suzanne
became the first 'Orphan of
the Nation' – an official but
mainly symbolic adoption
procedure – and was
nicknamed 'Mademoiselle
Nation'. The great simplicity
of the portrait on a
monochrome background is
characteristic of David's
portraits of this period and
embodies the very essence of
his genius. This picture
achieved a world auction
record for the artist.

Carle Vernet

The Arab Stallion Gazal
Signed and dated *1824*
Oil on canvas, 59.5 × 73.5 cm
(23½ × 29 in)
London £276,500 ($461,755)
20.XI.96

Vernet's career spanned some of the most dramatic events in the history of France and his works reflect this. Originally a painter of hunting scenes, he turned to satirical themes after losing his aristocratic patrons with the Revolution. His passion for horses and the effervescence of the Napoleonic epic led him to paint vast contemporary heroic scenes, but with the Restoration he turned to exclusively equestrian subjects. He learned to portray these animals in a new manner, no longer representing farm horses, but British and Arab race horses. The Orient began to appear in his work from the beginning of the nineteenth century and by the time this painting was completed, in 1824, it had become the height of fashion.

Eugène Delacroix

An Arab Scribe with a Seated Woman in a Moroccan Interior
Signed
Watercolour, 20 × 27 cm (8 × 10½ in)
London £221,500 ($363,260)
11.VI.97

In 1832 Delacroix accompanied the Count de Mornay on a six-month journey to Morocco, which was to become the most influential experience of his life. Fascinated by the light of the Orient, he developed a new colour palette, dominated by rich and bright shades. Up to thirty years after his return to France, Delacroix used the many sketchbooks he had filled during his journey and worked them into superb colour compositions such as this strikingly fresh watercolour, probably painted around 1846. This watercolour comes from the wedding album given in 1846 by the Orléans family to the new Duchesse de Montpensier to commemorate her marriage to the Duc de Montpensier.

Albert Anker
Die ältere Schwester
(The Older Sister)
Signed and dated *1867*
Oil on canvas, 81.5 × 65.5 cm
(32⅝ × 26⅛ in)
Zurich SF905,400 (£386,923;
$632,874) 4.VI.97

Albert Anker's most
important paintings all
originate from his creative
period of 1863–1901. This
example unites a number of
themes that characterize
Anker's work, such as
portraits of children, three-
quarter-length portraits of
young girls and the natural
occupations of a group
within a secure, home
environment.

Emile Renouf
Un coup de main
(The Helping Hand)
Signed and dated *81*
Oil on canvas, 152.4 ×
226.1 cm (60 × 89 in)
New York $1,102,500
(£672,525) 12.11.97

Un coup de main hung in the Corcoran Collection in Washington, DC, for over 100 years, and achieved further fame with its widespread reproduction in schoolrooms throughout the United States. Renouf first exhibited it in 1881 at the Paris Salon, where art critics devoted a special section of their reviews to paintings associated with *la mer*, the sea. Renouf's work contrasts with those of his predecessors Turner and Vernet, who depicted people as tiny figures dominated by huge seas and skies. Here, Renouf concentrates on the details of human activity, the journey over water serving as a metaphor for transition and change in life.

Jean-Léon Gérôme
Le derviche tourneur
(The Whirling Dervish)
c. 1895, signed
Oil on canvas, 73.7 × 95.3 cm
(29 × 37½ in)
New York $1,020,000
(£622,200) 12.11.97

This painting depicts a ceremony common – in different forms – to all dervish brotherhoods, in which the name of Allah is evoked. Surrounded by howling dervishes (*Bayummiyyah*) the whirling dervish (*Malawiyyah*) has taken off his black coat, the

symbol of death, but retained his hat, the symbol of the tomb, for the ceremony. The setting of this work is almost certainly the mosque of Ma'bad al-Riffa-i in the Eastern Cemetery, Cairo, and Gérôme prepared for it with quick idea sketches followed by careful studies.

Jean Béraud
Sur le boulevard devant le Théâtre du Vaudeville
Signed
Oil on canvas, 27.3 × 35.2 cm (10¾ × 13⅞ in)
New York $640,500 (£397,110) 23.V.97

Life on the *grands boulevards* was a favourite subject of Béraud's. Here the artist captures one of the most fashionable intersections of *Belle Époque* Paris, the corner of the Boulevard des Capucines and the Rue de la Chaussée d'Antin. Napoleon III and Baron Haussmann had planned for this area to be a luxury theatre district and, in the early 1870s, the block became home to the immensely popular Théâtre du Vaudeville. This area was also an important artistic centre, with the first Impressionist exhibition being held on the Boulevard des Capucines.

RUSSIAN ART

Ilya Efimovich Repin
The Cossacks of the Black Sea
Signed
Oil on canvas, 360 × 254 cm
(144 × 101½ in) unframed
London £441,500 ($737,305)
19.XII.96

The realist artist Repin
enjoyed considerable
success during his lifetime,
and remains the most
renowned Russian artist of
the nineteenth and early
twentieth centuries. This
painting depicts a traditional
Cossack boat or *chaika*
crossing a tempestuous sea.
The cargo of textiles on the
boat suggests that the men
aboard have raided and
plundered Turkish and
Crimean settlements along
the Black Sea coast. These
raids were common during
a period in the seventeenth
century when hero and rebel
Stepan Razin was attempting
to establish an independent
Cossack republic.

ART IN ISRAEL

Reuven Rubin
Rider with Bouquet
Signed in Hebrew
Oil on canvas, 81.3 × 66 cm
(32 × 26 in)
Tel Aviv $283,000 (£172,630)
26.IV.97

Painted in 1923, this work is
from one of the most
intensely creative periods of
Rubin's life. In this year the
artist had his first one-man
exhibition in Tel Aviv, he
published a set of woodcuts,
The Godseekers, and designed
theatrical sets and costumes.
Rubin's intense use of colour
and strong impression of the
Levant is the essence of his
work from this period. He
described his feelings at the
time: 'I feel the sap of creative
energy rising in me .... The
world is clear and pure to me.
Life is stark, bare, primitive.'
Rider with Bouquet achieved a
record price for an Israeli
work of art.

IMPRESSIONIST
AND MODERN ART

Vincent van Gogh
La Moisson en Provence
1888, signed
Pencil, reed pen and brown
ink, watercolour and
gouache on paper, 48 ×
60 cm (19 × 23⅝ in)
London £8,801,500
($14,698,505) 24.VI.97
From the Collection of the
late Mrs J. B. A. Kessler

Van Gogh arrived in Arles
from Paris in February 1888
and spent the spring scouring
his new surroundings for
suitable views to paint. The
subject of this watercolour,
the plain of La Crau,
fascinated him from the
moment he laid eyes on it.
The summer of 1888 was a
remarkable phase in the
artist's life. Not only did he
discover the power of colour,
he also flowered as a
draughtsman, producing
some of his most beautiful
works on paper. This
development was due in part
to his discovery of locally
grown reeds that could be
used to create thicker nibs
for drawing. The variation in
breadth and intensity of line
that he found he could
achieve enormously
increased the expressiveness
of his work. His ardent
admiration for Japanese art
was also undoubtedly an
influence in this, one of his
greatest watercolours.

Edgar Degas
Danseuses
1899, signed twice
Pastel on paper laid down on
canvas, 60.5 × 63.5 cm (23¾
× 25 in)
New York $11,002,500
(£6,821,550) 13.v.97

By the time Degas executed
Danseuses, his relationship to
the subject matter of the
pastel had altered
dramatically. Earlier in his
career, Degas' interest in the
life of the city had embraced
a broad diversity of subjects
including racing scenes,
laundresses, cafés and
brothel interiors, as well as
nudes and the world of
dance. In the 1890s his work
concentrated almost
exclusively on the nude and
the ballet. Paradoxically, the
increasing introspection
and withdrawal that
characterized Degas' later
years resulted in pastels that
are exceptional for the
richness of their colour and
the innovative handling of
the medium itself.

Edouard Manet
Le bal de l'Opéra
1873, signed
Oil on canvas, 36.5 × 28.5 cm
(14¼ × 11¼ in)
London £1,596,500
($2,682,120) 3.XII.96

A preparatory study for the
painting of the same name,
the freshness and
spontaneity of this canvas
provide an insight into the
gestation of one of the major
compositions of the last
decade of Manet's career.
Taking up Daumier's
injunction to depict
contemporary life ('*Il faut
être de son temps*'), Manet
visited the bars, theatres and
restaurants of Paris, where
he executed various direct
studies of exceptional verve
and freedom. Some were
later worked up into more
finished pictures in the
studio, *Le bal de l'Opéra*
being the first of the series
which included *Un bar aux
Folies-Bergère*.

Paul Cézanne
La Côte du Galet, à Pontoise
c. 1879–81
Oil on canvas, 60 × 75.6 cm
(23⅝ × 29¾ in)
New York $11,002,500
(£6,670,200) 12.XI.96

Cézanne was first attracted to the village of Pontoise when visiting Pissarro in 1872 and he moved nearby with his family shortly afterwards. The two artists developed a close, stimulating relationship, encouraging Cézanne to open his eyes to the world outside. The motifs of this picture, such as the narrow, receding road, the tall trees, the clusters of cottages and the variegated patchwork of fields, recall a series of landscapes Pissarro painted in 1867. It has been suggested that, in his paintings of this region, Cézanne achieved artistic maturity. He devoted himself to a structural analysis of nature, and aimed to make 'something solid and enduring' of Impressionism.

Gustav Klimt
Litzlbergerkeller am Attersee
1915–16, signed
Oil on canvas, 110.5 ×
110.5 cm (43½ × 43½ in)
New York $14,742,500
(£9,140,350) 13.v.97
From the Estate of Serge
Sabarsky

Klimt spent nearly every
summer between 1897 and
1916 on the Attersee with the
family of his model and
muse Emilie Flöge. A keen
sailor, he was one of the first
on the lake to own a
motorboat, and this painting
was probably executed from
a boat. Fascinated by water,

the artist spent hours just
staring at the lake, watching
the changing patterns of
light and colour. A
photograph taken of the
Litzlbergerkeller in 1899
shows how Klimt has altered
the structure of the tavern to
integrate it into his painting,
making it appear as though it

is floating in a tranquil
dreamscape. Unaffected by
time of day, light or shade,
this mosaic of colour
schemes and forms suggests
the infinite variety of nature
and the portrayal of the
continuous, incessantly
changing process of life.

Edvard Munch
Girls on a Bridge
Signed and dated 1902
Oil on canvas, 100.3 ×
102.2 cm (39½ × 40¼ in)
New York $7,702,500
(£4,669,600) 12.XI.96
From the Estate of Wendell
Cherry

Munch described the period
from 1902 to 1908, which
ended with his admittance to
a psychiatric clinic in
Copenhagen, as 'the
unhappiest, the most
difficult and yet the most
fateful and productive years
of my life'. It was during this
turbulent period that he

painted *Girls on a Bridge*, a
version of one of his most
popular and lyrical motifs.
The first version of this
subject, of which there are no
less than twelve subsequent
renditions, was painted in
1899 and saw the artist
moving away from the
anxieties of individuals in the

direction of the universal.
Whilst remaining true to that
theme, the present picture is
marked by a strength of
colour and boldness of
spatial delineation that make
it one of the most confident
of all Munch's paintings.

Egon Schiele
Bekehrung (Conversion)
Signed and dated *1912*
Oil on canvas, 71.1 × 81 cm
(28 × 31⅞ in)
New York $3,412,500
(£2,115,750) 13.V.97
From the Estate of Serge
Sabarsky

By 1911 Schiele had become
obsessed with the spiritual
importance of his work, and
wrote in a letter, 'I am glad
there are so few who can
recognize art. That is
constant proof of its divine
nature.' This painting shows
a monk or holy man, who

may be Schiele, and two
women, one of whom may be
his mistress Wally Neuziel.
Jane Kallir comments that
Schiele's paintings of this
time 'collectively portrayed
the exchange of artistic
enlightenment, personified
by a taker – the supplicant/

artist – and a giver – God the
father, Schiele's literal father
or his artistic father, Klimt'.
(*Egon Schiele: The Complete
Works*, New York, 1990)

Amedeo Modigliani
Jeanne Hébuterne au chapeau
c. 1919, signed
Oil on canvas, 93 × 53 cm
(36⅝ × 20⅞ in)
New York $9,572,500
(£5,934,950) 13.v.97

Biographies of Modigliani
offer little information about
Jeanne Hébuterne, the
artist's mistress and
subsequent wife, who
committed suicide two days
after Modigliani's death. She
met the artist in 1917 and, for
the next three years, was his
constant companion and
source of inspiration, sitting
for approximately twenty-six
portraits. This elegant
picture synthesizes the
characteristics of
Modigliani's later portraits:
the geometric simplification
of the female form, the
S-shaped curve of the body,
the elongated neck, the
spatulated nose, the pursed,
small mouth with sensuous
lips and the vacant, almond
eyes which prevent the
viewer from communicating
with the sitter, enveloping
her in an enigmatic and
impenetrable mood.

Kees Van Dongen
Femme au grand chapeau
1906, signed
Oil on canvas, 100 × 81 cm
(39½ × 31¾ in)
London £2,201,500
($3,676,505) 24.VI.97
From the Collection of
Charles Tabachnick

In 1906 Van Dongen moved
to the Bateau-Lavoir, the
Montmartre home of the
most avant-garde group of
artists of the time. Van
Dongen's studio was
opposite that of Picasso and
his mistress and muse
Fernande Olivier, the model
for this portrait and a
number of others. Painted
during the artist's Fauve
period, this work may be
seen as a response to
Matisse's *Woman with the
Hat* of 1905, now considered
one of the Fauve's pivotal
works. Whilst the conflict in
Matisse's work is achieved
by the apparent contradiction
between the wild handling
of the pigment and the
apparently bourgeois
subject, Van Dongen's work
celebrates the simultaneous
sensual appeal of vibrant
colour and female sexuality.

Alexej von Jawlensky
Stilleben mit Kulitsch
(*Still Life With Cake*)
Signed and dated 1905
Oil on board laid down
on board, 76 × 71 cm
(29⅞ × 28 in)
London £1,211,500
($2,023,205) 24.VI.97

From the Collection of
Charles Tabachnick

Jawlensky was one of a
number of Russian artists
who gravitated towards
Munich in the 1890s and
early 1900s. He studied at
the art school run by Anton
Azbè and travelled widely to

acquaint himself with
developments in post-
Impressionist and avant-
garde art. He met Matisse in
1905, and was also
influenced by van Gogh and
Gauguin. In his memoirs,
dictated to Lisa Kümmel in
1937, Jawlensky explained
that he chose to paint still-

lifes 'because I could more
easily find myself. I tried in
these still-life paintings to go
beyond the material objects
and express in colour and
form the thing which was
vibrating within me, and I
achieved some good results.'

Ernst-Ludwig Kirchner

Strassenzene (Street Scene) – recto

Kopf Gräf (Portrait of Gräf) – verso

1913 (recto) and 1914 (verso), signed

Oil on canvas, 70 × 51 cm (27½ × 20 in)

London £1,981,500 ($3,309,105) 24.VI.97

From the Collection of Charles Tabachnick

Street Scene relates directly to the monumental series of Berlin street scenes which are among Kirchner's most celebrated paintings. He first visited Berlin in 1910, and moved there in 1911. The metropolitan life in the city had a profound effect on the artist's choice of subject matter and style, as Wolf-Dieter Dube writes: '[Kirchner] was seized by the dynamism of city life. [He] discovered new pictorial forms unique to himself and was the first to render the feel of a modern metropolis' (*Ernst Ludwig Kirchner,* Marlborough Fine Art, 1969). Botho Gräf, whose portrait appears on the reverse, was an archaeologist and art historian who bought several examples of Kirchner's work.

Piet Mondrian
Composition
Signed and dated *39–42*
Oil on canvas, 72.7 × 65.4 cm
(29⅝ × 25¾ in)
New York $5,502,500
(£3,335,860) 12.XI.96

Mondrian left Paris for London in 1938 and settled in Hampstead. During the late 1930s he had begun to establish a new linearity in his work, yet, as conditions in London began to deteriorate and bombings became daily events, many compositions were left incomplete. In October 1940

Mondrian arrived in New York, at the invitation of the artist Harry Holtzman. Once established there, Mondrian transformed his previously unfinished paintings by adding bands and blocks of colour in such a way that his enthusiasm for the vitality of the New World could be perceived by all.

Yves Tanguy

Sans Titre
Signed and dated *27*
Oil on canvas, 115 × 81 cm
(45¼ × 31⅞ in)
London £529,500 ($884,265)
24.VI.97
From the Collection of
André-François Petit, Paris

By 1927 Tanguy was in
complete command of a
highly personal surrealist
language. He was
particularly close to André
Breton at this time, and
shared his fascination with
dreams, the unconscious,
and paranormal phenomena.
Yet, underlying the
biomorphic imagery of
paintings such as this is,
above all, the landscape of
Finistère, the westernmost
tip of France overlooking the
Atlantic where the artist
spent his childhood
summers. Tanguy's father
had been a sea captain and
Tanguy himself had worked
as a sailor. The sea remained
a constant source of
inspiration and the mood of
early surrealist works such as
this has much to do with the
silence experienced by
sailors alone on a vast
stretch of water.

CONTEMPORARY ART

Franz Kline
Crosstown
Signed, 1955
Oil on canvas, 121.9 ×
165.1 cm (48 × 65 in)
New York $2,202,500
(£1,365,550) 6.v.97
Property of CBS Inc.

This masterpiece has not
been seen by the public since
it was bought for CBS by
William C. Paley over thirty
years ago. *Crosstown* was
painted in 1955, a time of
great fruition for Kline, and
his paintings from this
period are marked by open
gestural compositions
crossing the canvas,
spanning all directions of
pictorial space. Energy is an
essential component of
Kline's black and white
paintings, and *Crosstown*
embodies this dynamism.
The spontaneous paint
application, expansive
composition and minimal
palette make this a
powerful celebration of
the urban landscape.

Mark Rothko
No. 19
Signed and dated 1960
Oil on canvas, 175.9 ×
175.3 cm (69¼ × 69 in)
New York $2,202,500
(£1,365,550) 6.v.97
From the Collection of
William C. Janss

The ability of Rothko to evoke
feelings both sacred and
private, expressive and
profound, through his art is
perfectly embodied by *No.
19*. Painted at the height of
his career, this work is the
quintessential expression of
Rothko's lifelong goal to
render the 'simple expression
of complex thought'. His
mature style eliminated
representations of form or
symbols and, in the use of
disembodied colour,
achieves a synthesis of the
physical and the spiritual.

OPPOSITE

Richard Diebenkorn
Ocean Park #88
Signed and dated 75
Oil on canvas, 254 × 205.7 cm
(100 × 81 in)
New York $1,267,500
(£785,850) 6.v.97
From the Collection of
William C. Janss

Diebenkorn's *Ocean Park*
series represents a major
contribution to American
abstract painting. The strict
formalism of *Ocean Park #88*
relates to the urban,
industrial structure of Santa
Monica, while the open
composition reflects the light
of the Pacific coast. The
artist's palette and reductive
compositions were
influenced by Matisse's
treatment of space and use
of saturated colour.
Diebenkorn here juxtaposes
control and expansiveness,
creating compositional
tension whilst celebrating
the California landscape.

Lucio Fontana
Concetto spaziale
1961, oil and gold paint on
canvas, 150 × 150 cm
(59 × 59 in)
London £529,500 ($878,970)
26.VI.97

This painting belongs to the
celebrated *Venezie* series of
twenty-four paintings that
Fontana executed in Venice
in 1961. In this series
Fontana translated his
impressions of the city and

characteristic aspects of its
architecture on to canvas.
Here, the use of thick red oil
is combined with a baroque
black circular composition
that echoes the cupole of
Venice's churches. A

sweeping brushstroke of
gold paint, ending in a few,
short, half-moon-shaped
swirls, is reminiscent of the
city's shimmering light.

Renato Guttuso
Studio e paesaggio
1961
Oil and collage on canvas,
200 × 320 cm (78 × 124⅞ in)
Milan L283,800,000
(£102,985; $168,828) 27.V.97

Guttuso was Italy's primary twentieth-century practitioner of social realism. A founder of the anti-fascist association Corrente and member of the Resistance during World War II, he used his paintings to protest against the injustices that surrounded him; the German occupation, Mafia and local Sicilian politicians were all targets for his work. Guttuso himself became a politician in 1973 when he was elected councillor for his home town and in 1976 he was made an Italian senator. This painting captures a moment of quiet in an artist's studio and reflects the influence of other artists, including de Chirico.

Gerhard Richter
Reisebüro (Tourist Office)
Signed and dated 66
Oil on canvas, 149.8 × 130 cm
(59 × 51¼ in)
London £452,500 ($751,150)
26.VI.97

Tourism was one of the new signs of affluence in Germany in the 1960s, a fact that was recorded and explored by Richter in a number of his early works. The inspiration for this painting was an advertisement for the travel agency Hapac. Resembling a photograph taken from a moving car or train, this blurred image alludes to the idea of movement, travel and tourism, and epitomizes the artist's masterful fusion of subject matter and style of execution.

Jean Dubuffet
Les Palefreniers
Signed and dated *Octobre 50*
Oil on canvas, 114 × 146 cm
(44⅞ × 57½ in)
London £661,500
($1,098,090) 26.VI.97

Unseen by the public for over thirty-five years, this painting belongs to the rare group of *Intermèdes* Dubuffet created just prior to his *Corps de Dames* series in 1950. A year earlier he had begun to experiment with building up layers of paint, then scratching into the surface to create an animated, almost sculptural work. Here, colour returns to his palette in a radiant flurry of reds, yellows, blues and greens. Dubuffet's choice of subject – *Les Palefreniers*, or horse grooms – underlines his continual fascination with motifs that reside outside the canon of traditional Western art.

Jean-Michel Basquiat
Untitled
1985–86
Acrylic, oilstick and collage
on wood, 208 × 308 cm
(78¾ × 118⅛ in)
London £287,500 ($477,250)
26.VI.97

A fine example of Basquiat's late work, *Untitled* combines various materials, elements and subjects and is constructed so as to unite texture, surface and imagery. The three-dimensionality of the wooden panels attached and hammered by the artist to the grid of wooden planks embue this painting with a sculptural dimension and presence. Its imagery and words all form part of the artist's vocabulary that consistently appeared in his work and became a personal iconography.

Matthew Barney

Transexualis (decline)
Walk-in cooler, formed and cast petroleum jelly decline bench, human chorionic gonadotrophin, silicon gel pectoral form and video monitors, 365.8 × 426.7 × 259.1 cm (144 × 168 × 102 in)
New York $343,500
(£212,970) 6.v.97
From the Collection of Boston Children's Heart Foundation, Children's Hospital

This installation, originally exhibited in New York, is a companion piece to *Transexualis (incline)*, which was shown in Los Angeles. *Transexualis (decline)* has at its centre a walk-in refrigerator containing a weightlifter's decline bench covered in petroleum jelly. In both cases, the artist performs the descent and ascent by climbing the walls of the gallery while nude. Video monitors show additional performances by Barney in which he adopts a number of different personae, including football hero Jim Otto and Hollywood starlet Lana Turner. These two installations explore the roles played by sex, desire and gender in society; while *Transexualis (decline)* may evoke a sense of desire, it operates as an antiseptic haven for solitary pleasure, free of contamination from the outside world.

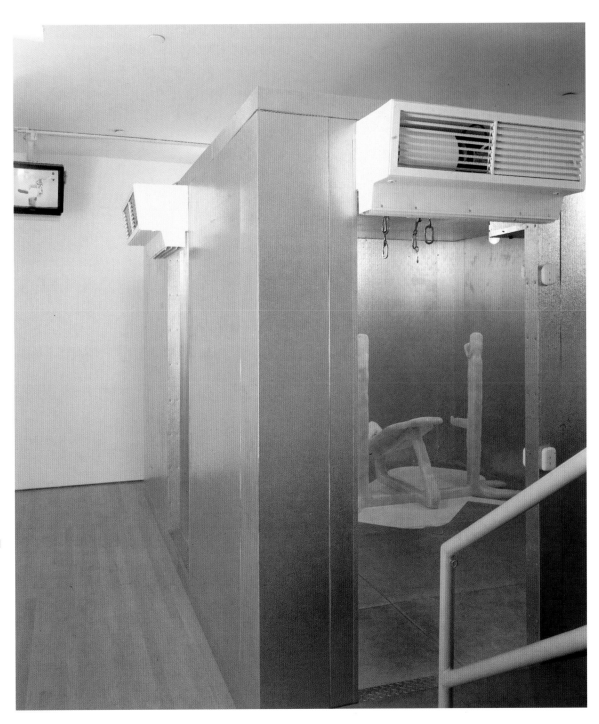

IRISH ART

Sir William Orpen
The Green Lady – Portrait of Amalia Errazuriz Vergara
1912, signed
Oil on canvas, 76 × 63.5 cm
(30 × 25 in)
London £221,500 ($365,475)
22.V.97

The Errazuriz family derived their wealth from silver mines in Chile, and were patrons of Picasso, Cocteau, Stravinsky and Diaghilev – the sitter herself was described by Proust as 'touched by art as if by heavenly grace'. She was also a friend of Mrs St George, Orpen's companion, and thus was introduced to the artist. Here, Madame Errazuriz is portrayed as a figure from the conflict surrounding the Flight of the Earls, when the last of the great Gaelic chiefs were defeated by the armies of James I and fled Ireland in 1607. This exploration of Irish identity, and its roots in the history and popular stereotypes of Irish life, represents a central theme in Orpen's work.

SCOTTISH PICTURES

Francis Campbell Boileau Cadell

Interior: The Red Chair
c. 1920–26, signed *F C B Cadell*
Oil on canvas, 61.5 × 51 cm
(24¼ × 20 in)
Gleneagles £109,300
($169,415) 20.VIII.96

This interior seems to have been painted when the artist was living at 6 Ainslie Place, Glasgow. One of the happiest periods of Cadell's life, it was during this time that he began to develop his style, using strong, bright colours to create bold patterns. Here, solid blocks of colour form a dramatic background to the focal point of the work – a red chair. The chair's appearance in the portrait on the wall characterizes Cadell's delight in reflections.

Childe Hassam
Dans le parc, Paris
Signed and dated *Paris 1889*
Oil on canvas, 32.4 × 41.3 cm
(12¾ × 16¼ in)
New York $1,267,500
(£773,175) 5.XII.96

Hassam immersed himself in the Impressionist aesthetic during a three-year visit to Paris in 1866. His earlier works from this trip reveal his continued interest in urban subject matter and his palette is more subdued. During the second half of his stay in Paris he began to incorporate the brilliant hues and broken brushstrokes of the French masters, as is evident in *Dans le parc, Paris*. Of this painting Richard Boyle writes: 'Hassam's brush has captured a bright and cloudless day, a Sunday sort of feeling in the kind of vignette William Dean Howells once called "the smiling aspects of life" ... [the] composition ... is based upon a stark vertical and horizontal structure – belied only by color and handling.... Even the color itself has a sense of movement.'

Mary Cassatt
*Sketch of Ellen Mary Cassatt
in a Big Blue Hat*
c. 1905
Oil on canvas, 61 × 55.9 cm
(24 × 22 in)
New York $552,500
(£337,025) 5.XII.96

Following a childhood spent
mostly in Europe, Cassatt
settled in Paris, where she
became a member of the
Impressionist group, and an
admirer of Monet, Courbier
and, particularly, Degas, with
whom she worked from 1879.
Her niece and namesake,
Ellen Mary, was a frequent
model of Cassatt's from
earliest childhood and in this
charming portrait she is
about eleven years old. A
popular visitor to her aunt's
house in France, Ellen Mary
inherited the Château de
Beaufresne when Cassatt
died in 1926.

Winslow Homer
*The Sutler's Tent
(Extra Rations)*
Signed *Homer* and
dated *1863*
Oil on canvas, 41.3 × 30.5 cm
(16¼ × 12 in)
New York $607,500
(£370,575) 5.XII.96
From the Collection of
Jeannette Scott

At the outbreak of the Civil War in America in April 1861 leading artists were called to the front to document impending battles. Homer, who was at the time a freelance artist for *Harper's Weekly*, was sent by the magazine to Alexandria, Virginia, where he spent several months documenting life on the front, collecting material for his first oil paintings. Homer's illustrations centre mainly on camp life rather than battles. A 'sutler' was a peddler of food, newspapers, tobacco and liquor, much in demand in the camps where rations were inadequate. Soldiers spent most of their wages on these items, as the government was not able to impose restrictions on the prices they charged, which led to inequity between the soldiers, as illustrated here.

OPPOSITE

Norman Rockwell
The Choirboy
Signed
Oil on canvas, 73.7 × 67.3 cm
(29 × 26½ in)
New York $717,500
(£437,675) 5.XII.96

Rockwell was the *Saturday Evening Post*'s chief cover artist for many years, and during this time made numerous references to his childhood in his work. This painting appeared on the cover of the issue of 17 April 1954 and recalls Rockwell's own days in a church choir. The model for the painting was a neighbour, Tom Chappell. Rockwell often used friends and family as models, believing that their faces were more expressive and open than those of paid models, and that they were more suitable to help him express his nostalgic view of 'clean, simple country life'.

Andrew Wyeth
Christina Olson
1947, signed
Tempera on panel,
86.4 × 64.1 cm (34 × 25¼ in)
New York $1,707,500
(£1,041,575) 6.VI.97

The artist's most famous
model, Christina Olson
appealed to Wyeth's artistic
sensibilities, possessing the
simple but expressive
features that suited his
naturalistic style. The two
also shared a deep emotional
connection which inspired
Wyeth on a personal level.
Beyond her individual
identity, Christina came to
symbolize for Wyeth her local
Maine environment and New
England heritage. Wyeth said
of this work, 'The shadow of
Christina's head against a
door has a ghostly quality,
eerie, fateful, serious, a
symbol of New England
people in the past – as they
really were.' In this portrait,
Wyeth removes extraneous
details of the setting to
convey the intense energy he
perceived in his subject.

Georgia O'Keeffe
The White Birch – Lake George
1925 or 1926, signed with the
artist's monogrammed
initials *OK*
Oil on canvas, 91.4 × 76.2 cm
(36 × 30 in)
New York $635,000
(£387,350) 6.VI.97
From the Collection of
William C. Janss

This work is one of a series of
the same subject which
O'Keeffe began painting on
the Stieglitz estate in Lake
George, New York, in 1921.
O'Keeffe first visited the area
in 1918 with Alfred Stieglitz,
the photographer whom she
married in 1924, and they
holidayed there annually
throughout the 1920s and

1930s. Drawing on the
motifs of her immediate
environment, O'Keeffe
painted the variety of trees,
leaves and flowers she found
on the property. Here, the
trunks of the birch are
strokes of white, the leaves
implied by broad areas of
green and yellow rather than
defined as separate forms.

Typical of O'Keeffe's
interest in combining
realistic observation and
abstraction, the line has
evolved to produce semi-
abstract shapes.

LATIN AMERICAN PAINTINGS

Ferdinand Bellermann
San Esteban
c. 1845, signed
Oil on canvas, 52.4 × 67.6 cm
(20⅝ × 26⅝ in)
New York $233,500
(£142,435) 29.v.97

Ferdinand Bellermann, born in Erfurt, Germany, was influenced by naturalist Alexander Von Humboldt, who had studied South America's magnificent geography and wildlife at the beginning of the nineteenth century. Like previous explorers, Bellermann was captivated by Venezuela's lush tropical topography. *San Esteban*, set in the mountains near Puerto Cabello, reflects the spirit of the itinerant painters who sought to capture the romantic landscapes of exotic lands. Most of Bellermann's paintings are preserved in the National Gallery of Berlin and in private collections in Venezuela.

René Portocarrero
Interior del cerro
Signed and dated *1943*
Oil on canvas, 79.1 × 66.7 cm
(31⅛ × 26¼ in)
New York $195,000
(£117,000) 25.XI.96

Interior del cerro achieves the goals of the modernist movement active in Cuba in the 1940s: in its swirls, its dramatic brushstrokes, its rich texture and colouration, the painting is a fusion of post-Impressionism and Fauvism that utilizes the material offered by a Cuban colonial interior. Portocarrero rejoices in the intricate visual possibilities of a screen, a flower stand, the dado and the rectilinear tiles that serve to highlight a flower arrangement in a pitcher and a still life of flowers and fruit.

Rufino Tamayo
Sandías
Signed and dated 0-51
Oil on canvas, 120 × 179.7 cm
(47¼ × 70¾ in)
New York $2,367,500
(£1,444,175) 29.v.97
Property of the Kathleen
Winsor Management Trust,
New York

In this monumental painting,
Rufino Tamayo reveals his
masterful use of colour while
exploring one of his favourite
and best-known icons, the
watermelon. The fruit is
symbolic; a staple of the
Mexican diet, it slices open
to reveal the green, white and
red of the Mexican flag.

Proudly Mexican himself,
Tamayo honoured his
compatriots by making such
familiar imagery a feature of
his work. In this seemingly
simple composition, the
fleeting moment of the
'still life' has been captured
just as the inviting delicacy
will disappear.

Miguel Covarrubias

George Gershwin, An American in Paris
1929, signed
Oil on canvas, 75.9 × 99.1 cm
(29⅞ × 39 in)
New York $244,500
(£149,145) 29.V.97
Property of CBS Inc.

At the age of eighteen, Miguel Covarrubias received a stipend from the Mexican government that enabled him to travel to New York where he swiftly achieved success as a caricaturist with *Vogue*, *The New Yorker* and *Vanity Fair*. Commissioned by Steinway and Sons as a rendition of Gershwin's trip to Paris during the 1920s, this painting was used to advertise the orchestral poem of the same name which premiered in New York in 1929. Covarrubias' style captures the vitality, fast pace and prosperous atmosphere of 1920s Paris. Gershwin, fresh from the prohibition of the United States, is depicted, holding a cigarette and apparently dazed, among the frolicsome and frenzied crowd.

Franklin Carmichael
Old Pine, Grace Lake
Signed and dated *1933*
Oil on canvas, 63.5 × 76.2 cm
(25 × 30 in)
Toronto CN$231,000
(£101,871; $166,089) 14.v.97

Grace Lake is in the La Cloche Hills region of Ontario, an area where Carmichael built a cabin and sketched regularly. He gave this painting to friends as a wedding gift, and it remained in a private family collection until its sale this year. His daughter, Mary

Mastin, has said that the lake was a constant source of inspiration for the artist, and Megan Bice, author of *Light and Shadow, The Work of Franklin Carmichael*, writes: 'The La Cloche paintings of the 1930s show the full development and

accomplished interpretation of Carmichael's ideas. He took as the basis of his subject matter the symbiotic relationships between the opposites of the natural cycle: the minute and the grandiose, the fragile and the hardy, creation and decay.'

AUSTRALIAN ART

Frank Jeffrey Edson Smart
*The Guiding Spheres
(Homage to Cézanne) II*
1979–80, signed
Oil and synthetic polymer
paint on canvas, 83 × 100 cm
(32⅜ × 39 in)
Melbourne AUS$112,500
(£56,250; $87,750) 19.VIII.96

The clear beauty and
importance assigned to
basic forms in *The Guiding
Spheres II* is representative of
Smart's mature output. This
is the second, tighter version
of a work that resulted from
Smart's visit to the major
Cézanne exhibition in Paris

in 1978. The dedication,
'Homage to Cézanne',
acknowledges Cézanne's
advice to artist Emile
Bernard to 'see in nature the
cylinder, the sphere and the
cone'. The unsettling
presence of the floating
spheres in the painting is

enhanced by the detail of
red inserts and plastic
mouldings, which appear on
the lane markers at Italian
autostrade toll points.

PRINTS

Rembrandt Harmensz. van Rijn
The Three Trees
1643, etching with drypoint and burin on paper
21 × 28 cm (8¼ × 11 in)
London £133,500 ($218,940)
5.XII.96

This has long been the most celebrated and highly finished of all Rembrandt's landscape prints, where the artist has used great refinement of line to suggest the heavy clouds of a passing storm. Despite its popularity, it is a very rare print.

Winslow Homer
Eight Bells
1887, signed
Etching on vellum, sheet
53.5 × 67 cm (21 × 26⅜ in)
New York $68,500 (£41,785)
7.XI.96

The sea was Homer's favourite subject. From 1882 to the end of his life in 1910, he lived in isolation on the coast of Maine. His best-known works emphasize the power of that sea and explore the fierce relationship between man and the forces of nature. It is telling that one of the most productive and formative periods for Homer as an artist was 1862, when he was sent by *Harper's* as a 'special artist' to record the Peninsular Campaign in second year of the Civil War. The composition of this etching distinctly informs the maritime theme with a warlike attitude.

Edvard Munch
Zum Walde
Signed, inscribed and dated
1918–20
Woodcut printed in blue,
grey-green, rose, black,
yellow and green, 60.1 ×
76.6 cm (23⅝ × 30⅛ in)
London £120,300
($200,901) 25.VI.97

This woodcut is made using
the same colour block as a
1897 version (Schiefler 100),
although this new
interpretation is cut to
change completely the
atmosphere of the subject.
Munch's work is
characterized by the
intensity and conviction in
his representation of
extreme psychological

states. The two versions of
this subject straddle the
artist's 'complete mental
collapse' in 1908. After his
recovery much of the
anguished imagery
disappeared and his work
became much more
extroverted. This calmer
reworking has been noted to
reflect Munch's more
positive outlook on life.

Henri Matisse

Jazz (D. book no. 22; *The Artist and the Book* 200; Rauch 171; F. bk no. 9)
Signed and numbered *33* from the edition of 250
Complete book, comprising twenty stencils printed in colours after collages and cut paper designs, with facsimile text by the artist, published by Tériade, Paris, 1947
Each page approx. 42.3 × 32.5 cm (16⅝ × 12¾ in)
New York $222,500 (£135,670) 16.v.97

Matisse was wholly committed to the art of the illustrated book, and the exceptionally striking *Jazz*, interweaving brilliant colours and simple combinations of paper cut-outs with Matisse's undulating handwriting, is the artist's masterpiece in this form. It is a demonstration of Matisse's invention of 'drawing with scissors' in tandem with drawing with ink. Handwritten lines are punctuated with sudden and precise clashes of colour forming a syncopated composition that Matisse held to be a visual counterpart of jazz music. Following publication of the book, Matisse commented, 'Jazz is rhythm and meaning.'

Andy Warhol
Mao
1972, signed and numbered
28/250
Ten silkscreens printed in
colours by Styria Studios,
published by Castelli
Graphics and Multiples, Inc.,
New York
each sheet 91.5 × 91.5 cm
(36 × 36 in)
London £33,000 ($55,110)
6.XII.96

Moving on from his
enormously successful
career as a commercial artist
(mainly producing shoe
advertisements), in 1960
Warhol began to make
paintings based on other
mass-produced images.
Campbell's soup cans and
Coca-Cola bottles proved to
be a sensational attraction.
He also embarked on
numerous series of pictures
of Marilyn Monroe,
Elizabeth Taylor and other
celebrities. For these he
favoured a silkscreen
process which allowed an
endless replication. He
sought this repetition as an
expression of defiance of the
idea of a work of art as a
unique expression of an
individual personality.
Warhol proclaimed, 'I want
everybody to think alike. I
think everybody should be a
machine'.

Jasper Johns
Flags I (F.173)
1973, signed, inscribed *'I'*
and numbered *29/65*
Silkscreen printed in colours,
on J.B. Green paper, sheet:
70.2 × 90 cm
(27⅝ × 35⅜ in)
New York $233,500
(£142,435) 9.XI.96

Johns, like Warhol, worked as a commercial artist in New York in the 1950s, and moved on in his art towards the representation of apparently banal subjects such as beer cans and coffee tins, thus becoming an inspiration for the (less painterly) practitioners of pop art. Johns himself described much of his work as being 'involved with the painting as an object, as a real thing in itself'. He therefore often used flags in his work as they, along with targets, maps, numbers and letters, seemed 'pre-formed, conventional, depersonalised, factual, exterior elements'. These objects in his paintings exist as 'clear facts' and do not have to be judged.

Samuel J. Miller
Frederick Douglass
c. 1852, stamped *S. J. Miller, Akron, O.*
Half-plate daguerreotype, with the original seals, cased, the case lined with velvet
New York $184,000
(£117,580) 2.x.96

Frederick Douglass, abolitionist and newspaper editor, is pictured as he appeared in the early 1850s, his life as a slave behind him and his career as one of America's leading anti-slavery activists on the rise. This image was probably made in 1852 when Douglass travelled to Ohio and

Pennsylvania on a speaking tour. Samuel Miller was known as the 'pioneer photographer' of the city of Akron and was praised for his ability to pose his subjects – a skill illustrated in this powerful image, the largest extant daguerreotype of Douglass.

Jacques Henri Lartigue
Renée Perle with Motoring Goggles
1930–32
Silver print, toned chocolate brown, 13.1 × 17.9 cm
(5¼ × 7⅛ in)
London £27,600 ($44,712)
2.v.97

This rare vintage print is one of a series given by Lartigue to Renée Perle during the brief period of their relationship between 1930 and 1932. Catching sight of her on a street, the photographer was immediately captivated by the former model. In Lartigue's account of their first meeting he says '. . . her charm disturbs me. I am afraid it always will. Renée is beautiful; she is tender; she is everything I desire. I live in a dream.'

LITERARY PROPERTY

An Apollo and Pegasus Binding for Giovanni Battista Grimaldi on Robert Estienne, *Dictionarium*
Paris, 1542
Binding 38.5 × 25.5 cm (15⅛ × 10 in)
London £221,500 ($363,260)
5.XII.96
Sold by order of the Trustees of the Bibliotheca Wittockiana

The pursuit and discovery of the man for whom these bindings were made is one of the great detective stories in the history of bookbinding. It was not until 1970 that Anthony Hobson solved the mystery, and revealed the identity of the original owner, Grimaldi, a wealthy banker from Genoa. The bindings were made by Niccolò

Franzese in Rome, *c.* 1545. The author of the *Dictionarium*, Estienne, was a controversial figure who became a 'condemned author' because of his Protestantism; the first three leaves of volume I, which bore his name, have been removed by the censor.

The Tragedy of Richard the Third:
with the Landing of Earle Richmond, and the Battell at Bosworth Field.

Francesco Colonna

Hypnerotomachia Poliphili
First edition, folio
Venice, Aldus Manutius,
December 1499
Milan L103,000,000
(£36,807; $60,339) 7.v.97

William Shakespeare

Mr. William Shakespeares Comedies, Histories and Tragedies. Published according to the True Originall Copies
London, Isaac Iaggard and Ed. Blount, 1623, first edition, folio 33 × 21 cm (13 × 8¼ in)
New York $250,500
(£155,000) 29.x.96

From the Victor and Irene Murr Jacobs Collection, sold for the Benefit of the President and Fellows of Harvard College

This first edition of Shakespeare's collected plays presents the first editions of eighteen plays, the only authoritative text of several

more, and superior versions of others previously printed in quarto editions. Sixteen of the 454 original leaves, comprising the title and fifteen other preliminary leaves, are missing, and have been supplied in photo-facsimile on a variety of seventeenth- to nineteenth-century papers.

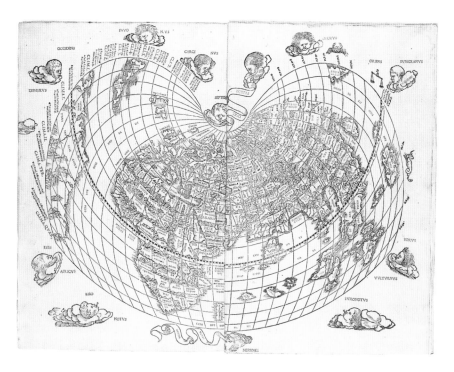

Claudius Ptolemaeus
Liber Geographiae cum tabulis et universali figura, translated by Jacobus Angelus; edited by Bernardo Sylvanus of Eboli
Venice, Jacobus Pentius de Leucho, 20 March 1511
Folio 43.7 × 29.5 cm (17⅛ × 11⅝ in)
London £44,400 ($73,704)
26.VI.97

This first Venetian edition is one of the earliest known examples of two-colour printing in cartography, with the major regional names printed in red and others in black. The maps demonstrate Sylvanus' acquaintance with recent discoveries, such as those made during the Cortereal and Vespucci voyages. The large cordiform

world map is the earliest of its kind, and only the second map in an edition of Ptolemy to show America (*regalis domus* and *terra laboratoru[m]*). It is also the first Western printed map to indicate Japan (*Zampagu Ins*).

Cornelius van der Myle
The album amicorum of Cornelius van der Myle
(or *Mijle*)
1594–1604
173 leaves
London £27,600 ($45,264)
5.XII.96

This album, with its elaborate inscriptions, coats of arms and emblematic illustrations, is a potent evocation of the world of European Protestantism in the 1590s. Cornelius van der Myle was a student at the University of Leiden who, after matriculating, collected these inscriptions from his professors and other

scholars as he travelled in Europe. Most of the inscriptions are in Latin, but others are in French, Greek, Hebrew, Syriac and Arabic. The volume includes forty-four coats of arms and sixteen watercolours of classical scenes. Myle has added later obituary notes to a number of the inscriptions.

Christoph Jakob Trew – Georg Dionys Ehret – Robert Furber

Christoph Jakob Trew, *Plantae selectae quarum imagines ad exemplaria naturalia Londini* [Nuremberg] 1750–73 – Georg Dionys Ehret, *Plantae at papiliones rariores depictae at aeri incisae a Georgio Dionysio Ehret* London 1748–62 – Robert Furber, *Twelve Months of Flowers* London 1730 3 volumes bound in 1, folio New York \$112,500 (£68,625) 3.VI.97

This is a major compilation of three eighteenth-century botanical books. Two are the principal published works of the brilliant botanical draughtsman and flower painter, G. D. Ehret. The connection between these works is London, where Ehret settled in 1732 after a period of European travel. Two of the works were printed in London; the third work is from drawings made by Ehret in London and sent to Germany where they were copied by engravers Johann Jacob and Johann Elias Haid.

Philipp Franz von Siebold and others

Fauna Japonica
Leiden, 1833–50
Five volumes with 402 lithographed plates, folio size 37.5–40 × 28–29.5 cm (14¾–15¾ × 11–11⅝ in)
London £35,600 ($59,452)
26.XI.96

Siebold was born in Germany, but worked as a doctor for the Dutch government, and was transferred to Japan in 1823. In addition to his immense contribution to Japanese medicine, he found time to satisfy his curiosity about the fauna and flora of the country. He built up a large collection of specimens, and, after his expulsion from Japan in 1829, he devoted himself to *Fauna Japonica*, which was issued in six parts over a period of seventeen years.

John James Audubon and the Rev. John Bachman

The Viviparous Quadrupeds of North America
J. J. Audubon, New York, 1845–46–48–51, first edition, 5 volumes of which 3 volumes folio and 2 volumes royal 8vo
New York $189,500 (£115,595) 3.VI.97
Sold for the Benefit of the United Jewish Community of the Virginia Peninsula, Inc.

This brilliantly coloured set of Audubon's *Viviparous Quadrupeds* was his great final work. It contains 150 hand-coloured lithographed plates of which the artist managed to complete seventy-seven drawings before ill health kept him from his work. The remainder were completed by John Woodhouse Audubon.

THE OBSERVATORY AT DELHI.

Thomas and William Daniell

Oriental Scenery bound with *Views in Calcutta* and *Panoramic Sketch of Prince of Wales Island*
London and Calcutta, between 1786 and 1821, first editions of 8 volumes in 3, large folio, 166 handcoloured aquatint plates, 6 aquatint title-pages and 1 hand-coloured etching
73.7 × 55.9 cm (29 × 22 in)
New York $277,500
(£169,275) 4.XII.96

Thomas Daniell and his nephew William spent nine years in India making studies, sketches and drawings for *Oriental Scenery*, widely recognized as the finest illustrated work on India, and another thirteen years producing the aquatints. The work, which depicts scenery, architecture and antiquities, inspired a cult for everything Indian in Britain, at the heart of which was the Royal Pavilion at Brighton. *Views in Calcutta* is

an earlier work by Thomas Daniell, and *Panoramic Sketch of Prince of Wales Island* is by William Daniell, after a drawing by Captain Robert Smith. It depicts the island now known as Penang in Malaysia.

Abraham Lincoln signature
'A. Lincoln – Springfield, Ill.
January 26 1861' written on
card mount at the foot of a
large, coated, or albumenized,
oval salt-print portrait, c. 13
or 20 January 1861
Print: 20.3 × 15.2 cm (8 ×
6 in); mount: 27.3 × 22.2 cm
(10¾ × 8¾ in)
New York $123,500 (£76,570)
29.X.96
From the Victor and Irene
Murr Jacobs Collection, sold
for the Benefit of the
President and Fellows of
Harvard College

This photograph was taken
by C. S. German two weeks
before Lincoln left
Springfield for Washington
D.C., a journey that took
almost a fortnight. Signed
carte-de-visite photographs
of Lincoln are relatively
common, as they were used
for pro-Union fundraising
activities, but larger signed
photographs are scarce.
Photographic portraits of any
size with an inscription in the
President's hand beyond his
mere signature are
particularly rare.

Sir Arthur Conan Doyle
Autograph manuscript of the
Sherlock Holmes novella *The
Sign of the Four*
Complete text, 160 leaves of
ledger-ruled foolscap, signed
twice, bound with 4
autograph letters to J. M.
Stoddart, 3 September
1889–17 March 1890
32.4 × 20 cm (12¾ × 7⅞ in)
New York $519,500
(£316,895) 4.XII.96

This is the most important
Sherlock Holmes manuscript
surviving, and is the only one
of the stories to be set from
autograph in the United
States. The book was written
as a result of a meeting in
summer 1889 with J. M.
Stoddart, a literary agent who
worked for Lippincott's in
Philadelphia. Doyle was
invited by Stoddart to a
dinner in London at which
Oscar Wilde was one of the
guests; at the end of the
evening Doyle had agreed to
write *The Sign of the Four*,
and Wilde *The Picture of
Dorian Grey*.

Sir Winston Churchill

Autograph letter signed to Jack Churchill, 19 June 1915
9 pages with autograph envelope signed and marked *'Secret'*
London £53,200 ($89,376)
17.VII.97

This confidential autograph letter was one of seventeen sold at auction in July 1997, all written to Major John ('Jack') Churchill (1880–1947) during the crucial period of the early years of World War I. The letter was written by Churchill to his younger brother, disclosing his feelings on the war situation and the disastrous Dardanelles campaign. The letter achieved not only the highest price for any letter written by Churchill, but also a world record for any twentieth-century letter written by an Englishman.

J.R.R. Tolkien

The Hobbit
First edition, 1937
London £9,775 ($16,128)
22.V.97

The first edition of this influential novel has ten plates and pictorial endpapers by the author. This copy is in the original pictorial dust jacket illustrated by the author, which is rare in such fine condition.

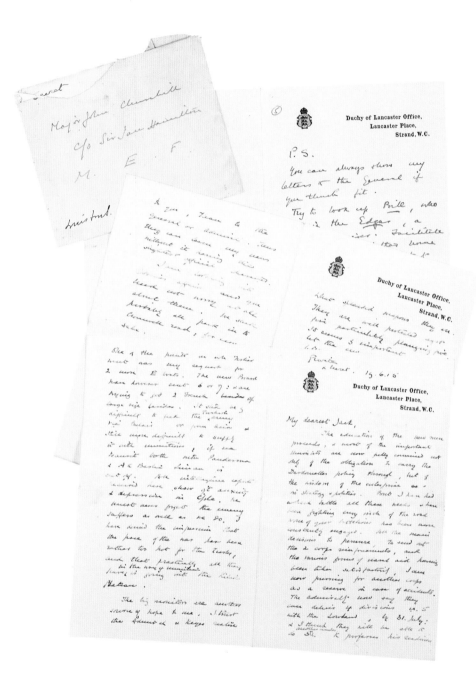

Igor Stravinsky
Autograph manuscript of
Stravinsky's orchestration of
Chopin's Nocturne in A-flat
major, Op. 32 no. 2
Signed and dated 1909
27 pages, small folio
London £81,800 ($134,152)
16.v.97

This orchestration was
commissioned by Diaghilev
for a production of Fokine's
ballet *Les Sylphides* on 4 June
1909. The orchestral writing
makes this manuscript as
extraordinary for its visual as
for its musical quality. At
times, the passages of
continuous fluttering effects
are so complex that they
allow room for only a single
bar of music per page.
Although based on Chopin's
Nocturne, the intricate
effects of the orchestration
are frequently the result of
pure compositional creativity
rather than representing an
expansion of the ideas
inherent in the original.

Ludwig van Beethoven
Autograph sketchleaf for the
Missa Solemnis
Probably Vienna,
February–March 1821
2 pages, oblong folio,
containing drafts for the
'Benedictus' and 'Sanctus'
London £67,500 ($110,700)
6.xii.96

Beethoven spent four years
composing the *Missa
Solemnis*, one of the
landmarks of his output.
While a number of sketches
exist for the 'Benedictus',
there are very few extant for
the 'Sanctus'. These
previously unrecorded, draft
pages are similar in size to a
desk sketchbook used by
Beethoven in 1821, known as
'Artaria 195', from which
several leaves are missing.

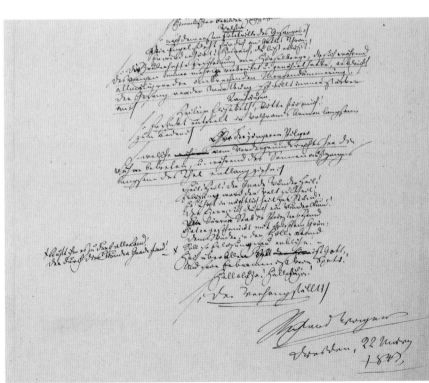

Richard Wagner
First draft of the libretto
for *Tannhäuser* (detail)
Dresden, January–March
1843
Autograph working
manuscript of 24 pages (4
blank) large folio, signed and
dated, with a presentation
leaf from Richard Wagner to
Wilhelm Baumgartner
London £84,000 ($137,760)
6.xii.96

A major discovery, this draft
was considered lost after it
was presented by the
composer to the Swiss
conductor Wilhelm
Baumgartner in 1852. The
manuscript has the character
and flow, as well as the
deletions and revisions, of a
first continuous working
draft. Although much of the
text is similar to the first
printed libretto, there are
numerous alterations,
including to the opera's most
famous moments, and the
final scene is quite different
from that performed today.

Jean Mansel
La Fleur des Histoires,
in French
Amiens, c. 1450–60
Illuminated manuscript on
vellum, 223 leaves, 41.5 ×
28.2 cm (16⅜ × 11 in)
London £342,500 ($558,275)
17.VI.97

This vast illustrated
manuscript of universal
history had remained
untraced since its last sale
in 1933. It is one of three
volumes probably
commissioned by the author
himself for presentation to
Antoine de Crévecour
(d. 1493), chamberlain of

the Dukes of Burgundy. The
other two volumes are in the
library of the Schottenstift in
Vienna. The present volume
has magnificent secular
miniatures filled with scenes
of battles, knights and
pageantry. They are close in
style to the work of the great
painter Simon Marmion.

The Children of the World Praising the Lord: **Large Historiated Initial from the Gradual of Santa Maria degli Angeli**, in Latin
Florence, *c.* 1427–33
Illuminated miniature on vellum, 30 × 23 cm
(11¾ × 9 in)
London £84,000 ($136,920)
17.VI.97

This extraordinary illuminated initial was brought into Sotheby's for identification in March 1997. It had been in the owner's family since at least 1856, and was in England by 1801. It is one of three initials that went missing during the Napoleonic invasion of Italy, cut from a sumptuous four-volume choirbook still in Florence. The two other missing initials had also been sold at Sotheby's (1945 and 1973 respectively) and the discovery of the third completes the set. The illumination has variously been attributed to Battista Sanguini (1393–1451), Zanobi Strozzi (1412–68) or even to Fra Angelico himself.

Girdle Book: Prayer Book, in
German
Passau, dated 1515
Manuscript on vellum with
decorated velvet girdle
binding, 196 leaves, 12 ×
9.3 cm (4¾ × 3⅝ in)
London £73,000 ($118,990)
17.VI.97

So-called 'girdle bindings'
were used especially for
covering portable
prayerbooks which were
carried around suspended
from their owner's belt or
girdle. The book's cover was
extended upwards above the
boards to form a kind of
attached bag tied at the top.
Girdle bindings are very often
shown in medieval paintings
and they must once have
been very common. They
were, however, extremely
fragile, and authentic
surviving examples are of
great rarity. Only twenty-three
girdle bindings are known.

**The Herbal of Dioscorides,
Isocrates and Galen**,
in Greek
Eastern Mediterranean, 15th
century
Illustrated manuscript on
paper, 119 leaves, 26.1 ×
19 cm (10¼ × 7½ in)
London £27,600 ($45,540)
10.XII.96

The science of botany
evolved from the medical
studies of ancient Greece.
This illustrated manuscript
Herbal in Greek appears to
have been unrecorded until
its appearance at Sotheby's
in 1996. It describes the
medicinal uses of 679
different plants and herbs.

The text claims to be based
on the work of the classical
physicians Dioscorides,
Isocrates and Galen. The
frontispiece here shows
Dioscorides and Galen
discussing the properties
of plants.

The Cockerell Hours,
in Dutch
Circle of the Master of Mary
of Guelders
North-eastern Netherlands,
c. 1420
Manuscript on vellum,
303 leaves, 13 × 9.5 cm (5⅛ ×
3¾ in)
London £1,002,500
($1,644,100) 16.VI.97
From the Beck Collection of
Illuminated Manuscripts

The Cockerell Hours takes its
name from its former owner,
Sir Sydney Cockerell
(1867–1962), who acquired it
in 1918. It is one of the most
important Dutch
manuscripts to appear at
auction in England this
century, and is among the
earliest major Dutch works
of art of any kind. It has
seventeen full-page
miniatures with scenes from

the life of Christ, often set in
the rather homely domestic
context that came to
characterize Dutch pictorial
art in later centuries. The
whole manuscript is
beautifully preserved in its
original binding. The
Cockerell Hours set a new
world record for the sale of a
Dutch manuscript at auction.

An Illustration from a Tantric Devi Series: the Goddess Worshipped by the Sage Chyavana
Attributed to the artist Kripal
Basohli, *c.* 1660–70
Gouache with gold and insect wing-cases on stout paper, 17.3 × 21.3 cm
(6¾ × 8⅜ in), London
£166,500 ($271,395) 23.IV.97

The sage Chyavana, an important figure in Indian mythology, sits on an animal skin in a grove of trees. The goddess, Devi, in her benign form, sits on a huge corpse and carries the symbols normally associated with the tranquil aspects of Vishnu – mace, discus, lotus and conch. Further leaves in the

series depict darker aspects of the Devi, where she also sits or stands on corpses. These illustrations confirm the enduring significance of goddess worship in Basohli, despite the efforts of the ruling house to promote Vaishnavite devotions. This work set a world auction record for a Pahari painting.

Firdausi's *Shahnama* with Preface, Illustrated and Illuminated Persian Manuscript on Paper with 58 Contemporary Miniatures

Copied by the scribe Jahangir
Persia, Shiraz, dated
AH 839–841/AD 1436–37
555 leaves, 25 lines to a page,
26.4 × 17.2 cm (10⅜ × 6¾ in)
London £315,000 ($500,850)
16.x.96

This manuscript of Firdausi's *Shahnama* is one of the finest examples of early Timurid manuscript production and typifies the high-quality work of the Timurid artists of Shiraz under the patronage of Ibrahim Sultan and his court. Although Ibrahim had died in 1435, the artist of this manuscript had probably worked in his atelier. The miniatures, which are attributable to three distinct hands, are untouched by later 'restoration'. The text of the manuscript is the version standardized by Baysunghur, Ibrahim's brother, with the exception of the preface.

**An Illustration to the
Bhagavata Purana: The
Wife of a Brahman
Sacrificer Offering Food to
Krishna Outside a Room
where Rites are Performed**
Mankot, *c.* 1730
Folio 27.3 × 20.3 cm
(10¾ × 8 in)
New York $34,500 (£22,080)
19.IX.96

This illustration is from a
Bhagavata Purana series
formerly in the Lambagraon
Royal Collection, Kangra. It
may have been given to two
Mankot princesses in the late
nineteenth century when
they married Raja Jai Chand,
ruler of Lambagraon
(Kangra). The amorous
content of the Krishna story
perhaps made it suitable for
inclusion in their dowry.

**An Illustration to the
Baburnama, Mughal:
Babur's Trip on a Raft from
China-fort**
Signed by Kamal Kashmiri,
c. 1590
24.5 × 14 cm (9⅝ × 5½ in)
New York $68,500 (£43,155)
20.III.97

This painting comes from
a dispersed manuscript of
the *Baburnama*, an
autobiographical work
written by the first Mughal
emperor, Babur. This first
illustrated version of the text
was probably completed in
1590, and was dispersed in
London in 1913; other leaves
are in the Victoria and Albert
Museum, London, the
Chester Beatty Library,
Dublin, and private
collections. Here, the
Emperor Babur, dressed in
orange, is seated on a raft
while a circle of men swim
frantically around a second
capsized raft.

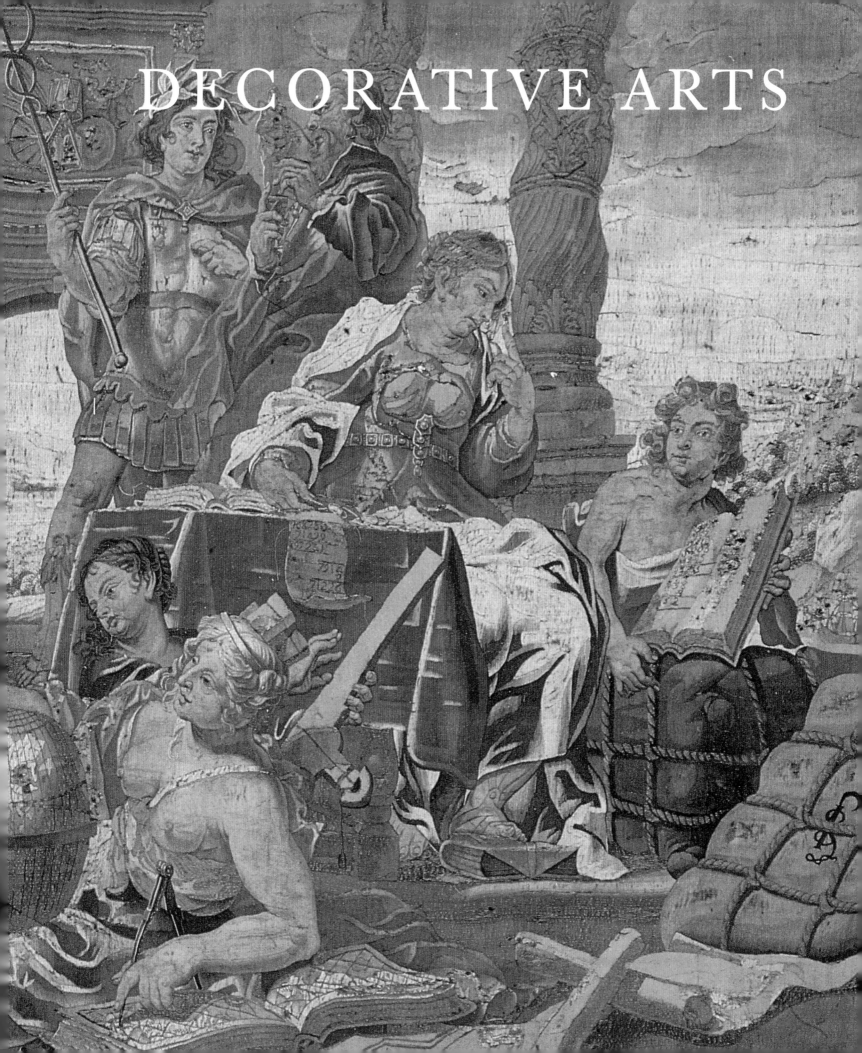

DECORATIVE ARTS

A Fatimid Rock-crystal Flask
Egyptian, c. 10th century
6 cm (2⅜ in)
London £45,500 ($73,710)
24.IV.97

A single line of *kufic* text is carved on the body of this small flask, proclaiming 'Glory and Prosperity to its owner'. Analysis of the interior reveals use of both a tubular and a solid drill rod, which is consistent with ancient drilling techniques. A group of toilet flasks of this type has been found and identified at Fustat in Egypt, an early centre of artisans and craftsmen.

A Life-size Gandharan Standing Figure of the Goddess Hariti
North-West Pakistan,
3rd/4th century
Grey schist, 1.71 m (67¼ in)
London £56,500 ($89,270)
17.X.96

The Mother-Goddess Hariti is depicted most frequently in Gandharan art accompanied by her husband Panchika. They were worshipped together as images of divine power, ensuring fertility and riches. Unlike other figures of Hariti, which are dressed in the heavily draped, classical manner, this image wears the kaftan, trousers and shawl that are often called Scythian or Iranian elsewhere in Gandharan imagery. The facial expression and treatment of drapery reflect late Roman influence.

A Kashan Lustre Pottery Ewer

Persia, dated *Muharram AH 660/November–December 1261 AD*
20 cm (7⅞ in), London
£67,500 ($106,650) 17.x.96

The quality of the painting, the highly vitreous glaze and the excellent condition of this vessel make it one of the most exceptional pieces of Persian lustre to appear on the market in recent years.

This is one of the earliest dated lustre vessels from the Ilkhanid period (1258–1335). Significantly for the history of Islamic ceramics, the sophistication of the ewer at this date clearly demonstrates

that production of lustre pottery continued throughout the thirteenth century despite decades of devastation wrought by the Mongols in their founding of the Ilkhanid Empire.

A Seljuk Incense Burner
c. late 12th century
Bronze, 18.1 cm (7⅛ in)
New York $85,000 (£51,850)
31.v.97

This elegant piece is cast in
the form of a partridge,
standing with its palmette-
shaped wings meeting over
its tail feathers. There is
elaborate *fleur de lis*
decoration on the back and
neck of the bird and its wings
are ornamented with
a guilloche rosette and
a geometric motif.

**A Tibetan Thanka of the
Dharmapala Yama**
c. 15th century
64.1 × 56.5 cm (25¼ ×
22¼ in)
New York $200,500
(£128,320) 19.ix.96

Yama, the ferocious judge of
the dead and ruler of hell,
stands on his bull vehicle
which lunges, wild-eyed, in
front of the stylized lotus
base of the throne. The deity
is highlighted by the fiery red
aureole behind his body
containing fifteen horrifying
members of his retinue,
including seven male Death
Lords, eight female deities
and the Great Mother
Goddess (Ma Mo Chen Ma),
as well as a Yamantaka figure
above Yama's head.

OPPOSITE

**A Gilt-bronze Nepalese
Figure of the Bodhisattva
Avalokitesvara**
c. 13th/14th century
39.1 cm (15⅜ in)
New York $277,500
(£174,825) 20.III.97

In Buddhist art,
Avalokitesvara is the most
frequently depicted of the
bodhisattvas – divine beings
whose primary role is to
provide guidance for others
still searching for
enlightenment. He is the
bodhisattva of compassion
and here stands in an elegant
pose, his hips swung gently
to the left and his right hand
extended in *varada* mudra – a
gesture of reassurance. His
distinctive emblem is the
lotus, seen here supported
on his left shoulder; its
stem was once held in his
left hand.

A Ukrainian Carpet
Mid-19th century
3.02 × 2.72 m
(9 ft 11 in × 8 ft 11 in)
New York $85,000 (£51,000)
13.XII.96

The design of this carpet
includes rose-hips, roses
and peonies as well as
stylized poppies. A three-
dimensional effect is
achieved by the pale,
feathered foliage at the rim
of each alternate wreath, and
the continuous border
repeats motifs from the large
central floral medallions. The
contrasts of muted green
and deep red are echoed in
cooler versions of the
colours: grey-blue, apricot
and pink. The lush floral
design of this carpet reflects
the opulent taste of the
eighteenth- and nineteenth-
century Russian court.

An Agra Carpet
North India
7.37 × 4.36 m
(24 ft 2 in × 14 ft 4 in)
London £95,000 ($154,850)
23.IV.97

Although initially Indian carpets were made on royal commission in small ateliers, when carpet weaving became a commercial activity much of the work was done in the country's jails. The earliest Indian carpets were often copies of the Maharaja of Jaipur's collection of Persian carpets and Agra swiftly became one of the cities renowned for the high quality of its carpet production.

An Isphahan Carpet
Central Persia, 17th century
4.88 × 2.16 m (16 ft × 7 ft 1 in)
London £133,500 ($212,265)
16.x.96
From the Collection formed
by the British Rail Pension
Fund

Despite earlier controversy
surrounding the place of
manufacture for this type of
carpet, Isphahan is now
generally considered to be
the likeliest source.
Established as the capital by
Shah Abbas I in 1598,
Isphahan was the epicentre
for all aspects of the arts,
including carpet and textile
manufacture, throughout the
seventeenth century and into
the eighteenth. This is a
sensational example of the
genre, in remarkable
condition and with its
luxurious colour preserved.

An Isphahan Rug
Central Persia, 17th century
1.9 × 1.27 m (6 ft 3 in ×
4 ft 2 in)
New York $310,500
(£192,150) 10.IV.97

This carpet, which was once
part of the collection
belonging to J.P. Morgan, is
one of a group of Isphahan
carpets woven during the
Safavid period, an era
described as the 'golden age
of the Persian pile carpet'.
The truth of this accolade is
borne out in the beauty and
harmony of design as well as
the superb condition of this
carpet. The burgundy field
colour, deep blue border and
design elements of floral
palmettes with serrated
outlines, scrolling arabesques
and eastern-derived
cloudbands are characteristic
of these Isphahans. This
carpet has an unusual
central bead in rose and sea-
green, which reappears in
the ivory inner guard border
as part of an atypical
repeating pattern of beads.

CHINESE ART

A Red Sandstone Figure of a Bodhisattva

Tang Dynasty (618–907)
60.4 cm (24¾ in)
Hong Kong HK$7,170,000
(£573,600; $932,100)
29.IV.97

This bare-torsoed bodhisattva is sculpted in high relief and shown seated in the *lalitasana* position on a rockwork plinth. The figure wears a celestial scarf around the shoulders, a jewelled necklace and a loose dhoti, which falls in folds over the plinth. His right foot rests on a lotus pod. The figure is very similar to those found in the Tianlongshan caves in Shanxi province.

An Unglazed Pottery Figure of a Caparisoned Fereghan Stallion
Tang Dynasty
Height 89.5 cm (35¼ in)
New York $937,500
(£590,625) 19.III.97

This large and superbly modelled stallion is a companion piece to a mare, also sold at Sotheby's in 1988. The precise anatomical detailing of the stallion is exceptional and the graceful yet powerful head and neck are particularly fine. Breast and crupper straps hold a saddlecloth in place, which has been roughened to simulate fur. The brick-red pigment of the cloth creates a strong contrast to the pale buff colour of the horse.

Walter Spies
Landscape
c. 1927–42
Oil on canvas, 71.5 × 59.5 cm
(28¼ × 23½ in)
Singapore S$1,103,750
(£485,650; $783,662)
29.III.97

The vision of Russian-born German artist Walter Spies was responsible for the development of a unique Balinese school of painting. Spies was struck by the country's culture, customs and, above all, its spirituality on his first visit to Bali in 1927. Here, the dramatic contrast of light and shadow and the absence of people or animals imbue the painting with a sense of this spirituality. The image of the volcanoes in the lake further symbolizes the spirit of Bali, and points to the origins of the country's fertile soil.

Zhu Yuanzhi (Yun Gee)
Bridge in Summer
c. 1940
Oil on canvas, 81 × 101.5 cm
(31⅞ × 40 in)
Taipei NT$4,230,000
(£966,111; $1,565,100)
13.IV.97

Zhu was born in Guangdong in 1906 and moved to San Francisco with his family when he was fifteen. He studied at the California School of Fine Arts for two years and pursued avant-garde colour theory under his friend and mentor Otis Oldfield. Zhu moved to Paris in 1928 where he held solo exhibitions in leading galleries. Upon his return to New York his work appeared in a major exhibition for American muralists and painters in the Museum of Modern Art in 1932.

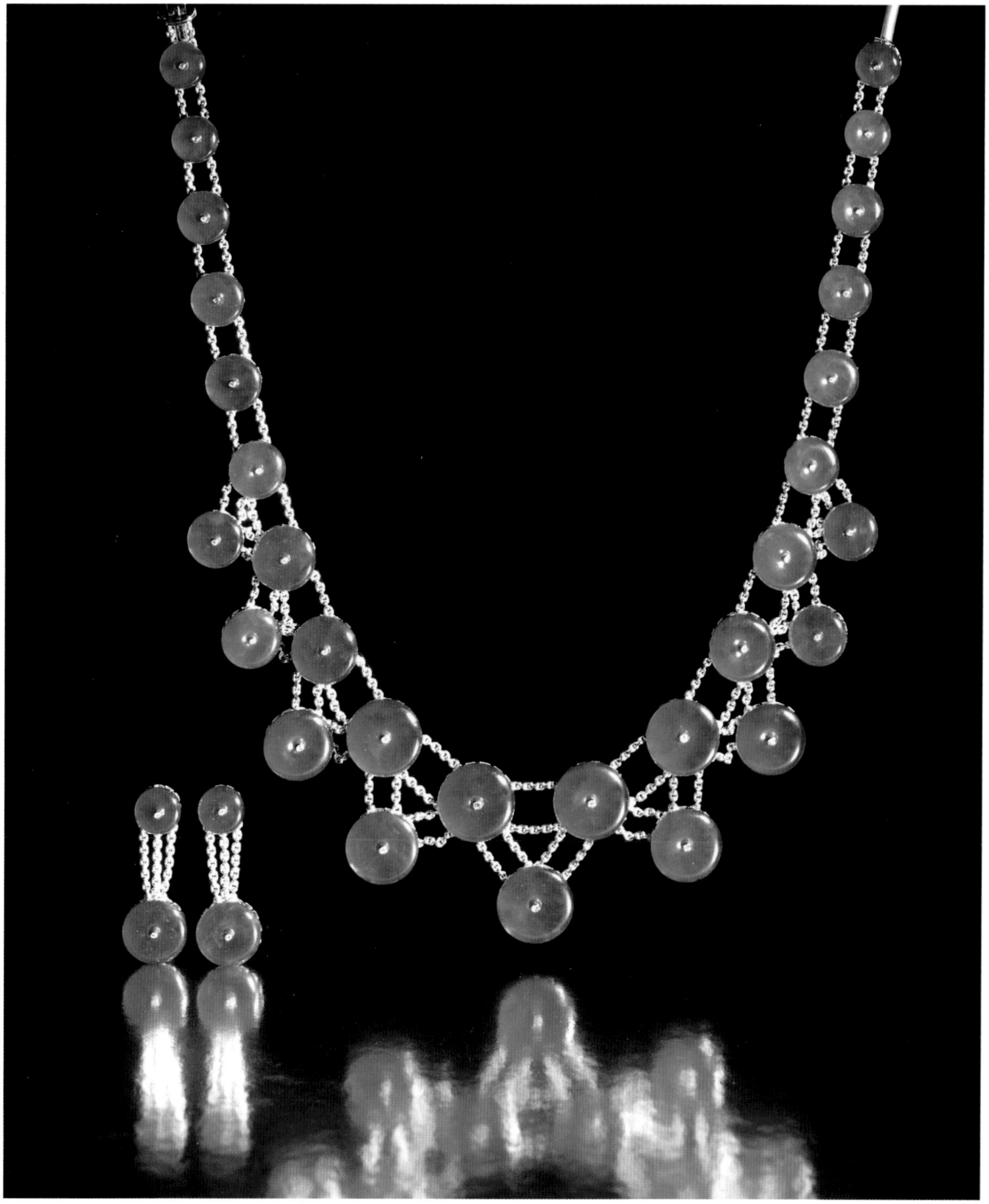

A Jadeite Huaigu Necklace and Pair of Matching Earrings
Diameter of necklace huaigu approximately 1.05 to 1.75 cm (3/8 to 11/16 in); diameter of earring huaigu approximately 1.03 and 1.5 cm (3/8 and 5/8 in)
Hong Kong HK$3,980,000 (£318,400; $517,400) 30.IV.97

This necklace is fashioned as a swag of twenty-nine brilliant emerald-green highly translucent huaigu joined by simple oval links. The matching earrings, of an equally rich colour and fine translucency, are mounted in eighteen-carat white gold.

A Jadeite and Diamond Pendant Brooch
Cabochon 2.18 × 2.58 × 1.07 cm (7/8 × 1 × 3/8 in)
Hong Kong HK$3,430,000 (£274,400; $445,900)
6.XI.96

An oval, apple-green cabochon is surrounded here by openwork decoration above a flexible fringe of sixty-nine diamonds.

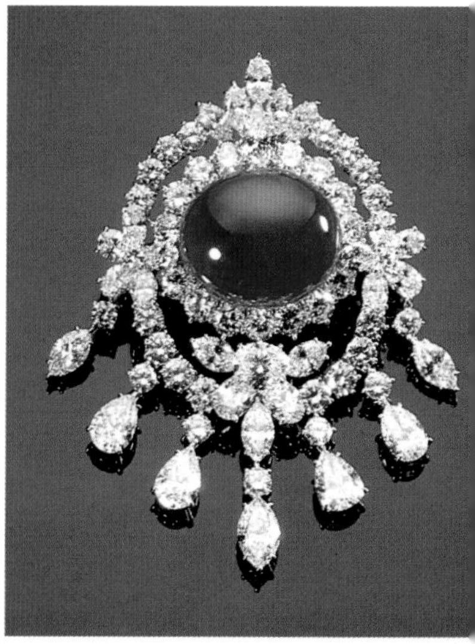

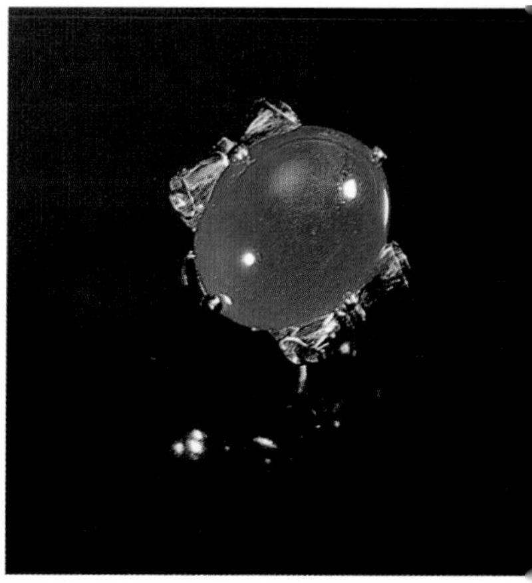

A Jadeite Cabochon Ring
Cabochon 2.14 × 1.8 × 1.2 cm (7/8 × 3/4 × 1/2 in)
Hong Kong HK$3,760,000 (£300,800; $488,800)
6.XI.96

The scrolled platinum mounting of this ring is set with a large, bright emerald-green cabochon.

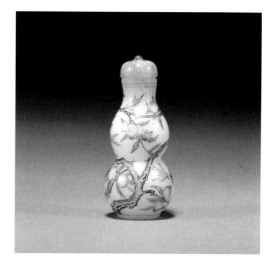

A *Huanghuali* folding horseshoe-back armchair, *Yuanhoubei Jiaoyi*

17th century
Height approximately
99.1 cm (39 in), overall
width 78.7 cm (31 in)
New York $453,500
(£290,705) 18.IX.96

There are probably fewer than thirty examples of folding horseshoe-back armchairs in existence. This *jiaoyi*, bound both in intricate damascened iron mounts and brass mounts, is the mate to one in a Beijing collection. The slender 'U'-shaped crestrail has outscrolled handgrips

beneath which are pierced dragon-form brackets, and the crooks of the arms also have dragon decorated brackets. The bowed rectangular splat is carved with a double-dragon cloud medallion.

OPPOSITE, FROM TOP

An Imperial Enamelled Glass Miniature Double-Gourd Snuff Bottle
Blue enamel four-character mark and period of Qianlong (1736–95), Beijing Palace Workshop
3.8 cm (1½ in)
Hong Kong HK$1,670,000 (£133,600; $217,100) 28.IV.97

Ding Erzhong
An Inside-painted Snuff Bottle
Signed and dated to the year *yiwei* (1895)
6.3 cm (2½ in)
New York $32,200 (£19,964) 17.III.97

A Yellow Glass Snuff Bottle
Qianlong (1736–95), attributed to the Imperial Glass Factory
6.4 cm (2½ in)
New York $41,400 (£25,668) 17.III.97

A Biscuit Figure of a Tiger
Kangxi (1662–1722)
Length 93 cm (36½ in), height 42 cm (16½ in)
London £364,500 ($601,425) 12.XI.96

This powerfully modelled tiger has teeth, fangs and tongue of rouge-de-fer, and the whole figure is washed in yellow enamel, with painted fur markings. The rump is pierced for insertion of the long tail. No other examples of this model have been published, although a comparable pair of leaping leopards were sold at Sotheby's, Monte Carlo in 1984.

A 'Tea Production' Punch Bowl
Qianlong, *c.* 1765
39.5 cm (15½ in), London £73,000 ($118,990) 8.IV.97

A continuous landscape encircling this bowl records the process of tea production. The various scenes show the tea being picked, dried, sold and shipped. Chinese and European figures outside a warehouse haggle over the price of the tea, while the buildings that surround them bear signs reading 'Happily we sail abroad' and 'Busy trade brings prosperity to Canton'.

KOREAN ART

Four Assemblies of Buddha
Inscribed with reign and
cyclical date corresponding
to AD 1562
Hanging scroll; gold and
colours on silk, mounted on
brocade, 90.5 × 74 cm
(35⅝ × 29⅛ in)
New York $717,500
(£452,025) 18.III.97

One of the few surviving
Buddhist examples from the
Choson Dynasty
(1392–1910), this important
painting was discovered to
be a unique example
illustrating a hitherto unseen
iconography. In addition to
its pristine condition, it bears
a detailed inscription
recording the date and
donor. Heralding a
significant addition to the
scholarship of Korean
Buddhist paintings, it set a
world record for any Choson
painting at auction.

JAPANESE ART

Hasegawa Tonin
Waterfowl in a Winter Landscape
Early 17th century
Six *fusuma* (four illustrated) mounted as three two-panel screens; ink, colour and gold leaf on paper, each screen approximately 160.7 × 167.6 cm (63¼ × 66 in) and 160.3 x 168.3 cm (63⅛ x 66¼ in)
New York, sold in two lots: four *fusuma* $420,500 (£269,120) and two *fusuma* $112,500 (£72,000) 20.IX.96

These six large-scale paintings are part of an original set of twelve. Once extending over 11 m (36 ft), the entire suite depicted a panoramic view of waterfowl in a winter landscape, set off against a background of reflective gold foil. The paintings are believed to have been commissioned *c.* 1617 for the castle at Akashi in the western part of Japan's main island of Honshu, where they were mounted as a wall of sliding doors.

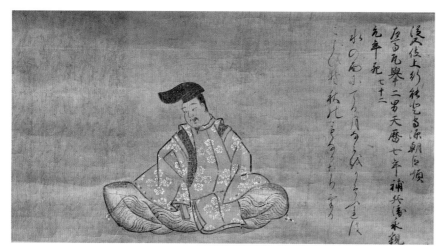

Anonymous

The Poet Minamoto no Shitago
14th/15th century
Hanging scroll, ink and colour on paper, mounted on brocade, 25.4 × 47 cm (10 × 18½ in)
New York $79,500 (£50,880)
20.IX.96

This hanging scroll is a fragment from a handscroll illustrating the Thirty-Six Immortal Poets, of whom Minamoto no Shitago (912–84) was one. Grandson of Emperor Saga, he devoted most of his life to the study of Chinese and Japanese literature, and is well known as the publisher of *Wamyoruijusho*. The inscription to the right of Minamoto's portrait contains his name, title, biography and a thirty-two-syllable *waka* poem.

RIGHT

Totoya Hokkei

The First Katsuo of the Season
Unsigned with a square red seal *Hokkei*, early 19th century
Hanging scroll, ink, colour and gofun on silk, 108 × 54.8 cm (42½ × 21½ in)
London £45,500 ($75,075)
13.XI.96

Originally a fishmonger, Hokkei later adopted the artistic name Totoya, which means fish shop. In this painting he illustrates one of the high points of early summer in Edo, when the first *katsuo* (bonito) are caught and eaten raw with *wasabi* (Japanese mustard) and soy sauce. The first bonito was the favourite subject of a number of artists; here it is accompanied by twelve verses written by members of an Edo poetry circle.

A Kakiemon Porcelain Model of a White Elephant

c. 1660–90

25.4 × 28.3 cm (10 × 11⅛ in)

New York $222,500

(£137,950) 21.iii.97

Its head lifted and turned to the left, this elephant has raised its curling trunk high. The open mouth reveals a pointed red tongue between rows of sharp and jagged teeth and the crescent-shaped eyes are below arched eyebrows delineated in black enamel. The animal's saddle-cloth is decorated with *karakusa* in blue, black and iron-red enamels bound with a tasselled cord round its girth.

Anonymous

Kamo Horse Race

18th/19th century

Pair of six-fold screens, ink, colour and gold leaf on paper, mounted on brocade, each screen 121.9 × 295.9 cm (48 × 116½ in)

New York $101,500

(£62,930) 21.iii.97

Kamigamo shrine (Kamo Betsurai Jinja) is a Shinto Temple located in Kamo, south of Kyoto. A horse race, depicted here, is held annually at the shrine on 5 May, the festival of Boy's Day.

Shibata Zeshin
A Four-case Metallic Green Lacquer Inro with Ivory Manju
19th century, signed
7.6 cm (3 in)
London £47,700 ($78,228)
18.VI.97
From the Raymond and Frances Bushell Collection of Inro and Lacquer

This inro has a dark metallic green ground, simulating old corroded bronze, which has been decorated with arrowroot leaves in gold, silver, carmine, *benigara*, bright and black *hiramakie*. The details are inlaid with *aogai*, and the design is continued on the reverse. The ivory *manju* is decorated with a wood sorrel design, laquered in gold and colours.

Kinkozan
A Satsuma Earthenware Vase
Signed *Dai Nihon Kyoto Awata Kinkozan zo*
Meiji period (1868–1912)
30.5 cm (12 in)
London £18,400 ($29,808)
10.IV.97

The pale ground of this vase has been decorated with a painted *henrinsha* (waterwheel) pattern. Bands of flowering cherry surround three panels, each differently painted with a warrior on horseback. The body of the vase is moulded and pierced, and the neck and foot are decorated and gilded. Awata was the Kyoto suburb in which the Kinkozan workshop was situated.

TRIBAL ART

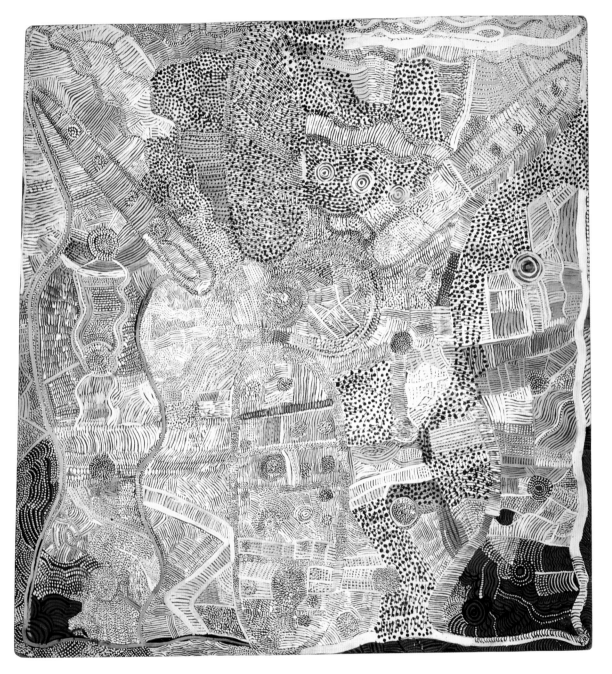

Johnny Warangkula Tjupurrula
Water Dreaming at Kalipinypa
1972
Synthetic polymer powder paint on composition board, 75 × 80 cm (29½ × 31½ in)
Melbourne AUS$206,000 (£90,640; $152,440) 30.VI.97
From the Tim Guthrie Collection

The Dreamtime is an Aboriginal story of the Creation and a Dreaming is a supernatural ancestral totem that imbues every facet of life, connecting the individual to the land of his conception. Kalipinypa is the site over which artist Tjupurrula has authority; it is a storm centre and 'Water or Rain Dreaming' totemic site. All features of the area are associated with the Creation time: sandhills are clouds, some outcrops are lightning, others are hailstones, and so on. Here, emphasis is given to the area's plant growth, in particular that of the wild raisin, shown as black dots on white lines. This painting is an exceptional example of the first 'Western Desert' paintings produced at Papunya in 1971–72, the seminal works that inspired the 'dot' painting movement that flourishes throughout Australia today. *Water Dreaming at Kalipinypa* set a world auction record for Aboriginal art.

Benin Bronze
Leopard Head
Middle period (17th century)
Height 23.5 cm (9¼ in)
New York $222,500
(£131,275) 21.XI.96

This head and its companion
piece at the Metropolitan
Musem of Art in New York
are the only known free-
standing leopard heads of
this quality. The floral
guilloche motif is likely to be
the result of European
influence in Benin, and was
probably introduced by the
Portuguese. The head is
spherical, and the almond-
shaped eyes have prominent
vertical pupils. One of the
leaf-shaped ears has broken
off, and the whole head is
covered with the floral
pattern overlaid with spots
in low relief.

Olowe
Yoruba House Post
1.8 m (71 in)
New York $354,500
(£209,155) 21.XI.96

Olowe of Ise (d. 1938) was
one of the greatest Yoruba
carvers of this century. He
worked for the King of Ise, a
town in southern Ekiti,
carving veranda posts,
doors, masks and bowls.
This post is composed in two
parts, showing a female
supporting a male astride a
horse. The male carries a
spear and flywhisk, the
implements of his authority,
and the female is flanked by
two attendants carrying
gunpowder containers. A
thick patina of layered
pigments in red, white and
indigo is overlaid by a dark,
encrusted patina. On its sale,
this post reached a record
price for a Yoruba work of art.

PRE-COLUMBIAN ART

Mayan Jade Figure of a Seated Lord

Early Classic, *c.* AD 250–450
Height 18.4 cm (7¼ in)
New York $332,500
(£202,825) 28.v.97

The Maya and Olmec considered jade the most precious of all stone substances. Representing life-giving water and vegetation, lightning and rain, the symbolic power of jade imbued every carving with supernatural significance. This imposing figure also conveys authority and rulership through its body markings, posture and accoutrements – all central concerns in Mayan religious ideology.

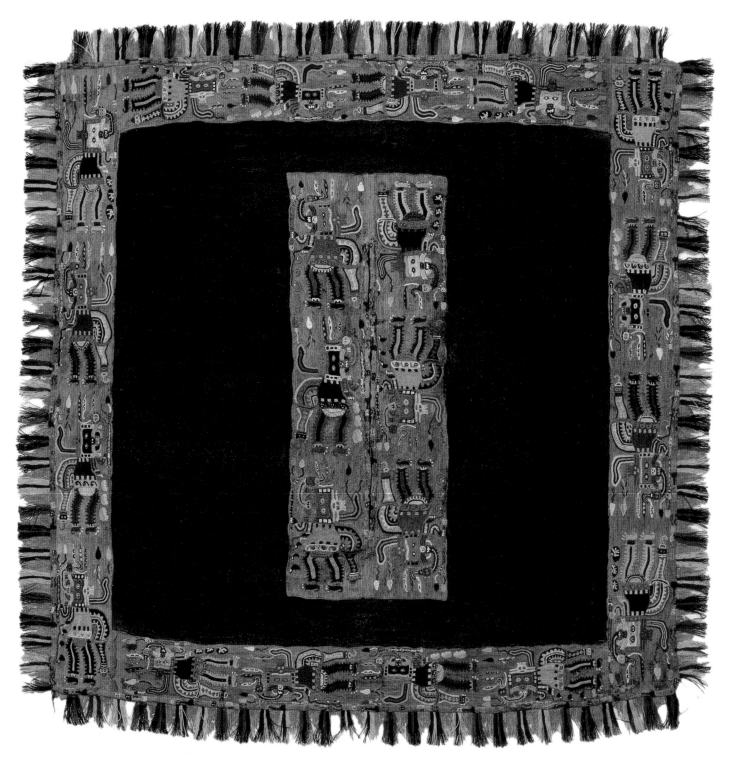

Late Paracas Embroidered Small Poncho
Paracas Necropolis,
c. 200 BC–AD 100
Camelid wool, 81.3 × 80 cm
(32 × 31½ in)
New York $398,500
(£243,085) 28.v.97
From the Estate of Mrs
Hans Hofmann

One of the relatively few complete *ponchito* types, this textile is a fine example of the detailed block colour-weaving style of later Necropolis funerary bundles. The layering of the funerary bundle is probably a metaphor for the bundle as a growing seed, the garment size and type relating to the life cycle of the deceased in the afterlife. These textiles can be read as 'texts' of the Paracas culture, the repeated images acting both as words and pictures.

A Tlingit Ceremonial Coat, Chilkat
Mountain goat's wool, cedar bark fibre and possibly commercial yarn, width across the arms 1.56 m (61½ in); length 1.19 m (47 in)
New York $497,500 (£303,475) 4.VI.97
Property of Adelaide DeMenil

This richly coloured coat has a stylized heraldic crest pattern representing a brown bear. A column of alternating faces form the animal's body and appear to be representations of the Bear, the mythological Tlingit woman who married him and their cub child. Two additional faces near the neck represent the Bear's ears, and the mouth is indicated by five human faces across the front. The reverse of the coat has a classic geometric pattern and a totemic animal mask at the shoulders.

A Nuu-Chah-Nulth (Nootka) Face Mask
Probably 18th century
Wood and human hair,
height 26.5 cm (10 7/16 in)
New York $525,000
(£320,250) 4.VI.97
Property of Adelaide
DeMenil

Depicted with a voracious
expression, this mask is
painted with red vermilion,
black and white pigment and
marked with small dotted
patterns and scalloped
decoration. The tufts of
human hair are secured by
wood pegs inserted across
the crown.

ANTIQUITIES

A Sasanian Silver-gilt Vase
6th–7th century AD
Height 17 cm (6¹¹/₁₆ in)
New York $893,500
(£536,100) 17.XII.96

It is probable that this Sasanian vessel was used to hold wine during court celebrations, such as the festival of Nauruz that took place in spring. The pear-shaped body is decorated with a lozenge-patterned framework containing, in the upper and lower areas, a lion, tiger, plants and various birds. Music and dancing characterize the activities of the figures in the central lozenges, with a lute and double flute being played while a woman dances, playing a pair of castanets, and another holds a cluster of grapes.

**An Egyptian Graywacke
Figure of a Kneeling Priest**
Late Period, 30th Dynasty,
c. 380–342 BC
35.4 cm (14 in)
London £309,500 ($507,580)
12.VI.97
Property from the Collections
of the Earls of Warwick

This important Egyptian
sculpture was formerly in the
collection of Henry Salt
(1780–1827) who was British
Consul General in Egypt. He
amassed three collections of
Egyptian antiquities; the first
was acquired by the British
Museum, the second by
Charles X, King of France,
and the third was sold at
Sotheby's in a seven-day sale
in 1835. This sculpture
formed part of the third
collection and fetched £60.

**A Sumerian Limestone
Votive Plaque**
Early Dynastic II,
c. 2700–2600 BC
26 × 25 cm (10¼ × 9⅞ in)
London £177,500 ($291,100)
12.VI.97
From the Erlenmeyer
Collection

This plaque belongs to a group of perforated wall plaques that are believed to have been set vertically into the wall next to the door jamb. A circular or square peg would be inserted into the central hole with a rope wrapped round it and then attached to the door. The

decoration on this plaque is arranged in three registers. The upper register is believed to represent the Sumerian ruler and his wife. The lower register shows four seated figures in a boat; the second figure holding a conical vessel may also represent the ruler.

A Cycladic Marble Figure of a Goddess

Early Bronze Age II, early
Spedos, *c.* 2600–2500 BC
Height 22.2 cm (8¾ in)
New York $178,500
(£108,885) 31.v.97

This figure stands with her
legs bent slightly at the knees
and forearms resting
beneath her breasts. She has
a long, slightly tapering neck
and a slender lyre-shaped
head on which the straight,
wedge-shaped nose merges
imperceptibly into the high
arc of the forehead.
Traces of red and black
pigment remain, indicating
facial features.

GARDEN STATUARY

A Marble Figure of a Spaniel
Late 19th century, signed *M. Muldoon & Co. Lou L.N*
Height 73.7 cm (29 in)
New York $12,650 (£7,716)
15.VI.97

This appealing dog wears a collar inscribed JESSIE, which suggests that the figure was made on commission as a memorial for a beloved pet. The spaniel sits in a lifelike attitude, alert and playful, beside a basket amidst roses.

A Doulton Stoneware Fountain
Probably modelled by George Tinworth, impressed *Doulton, Lambeth, c. 1890*
Height of fountain 137 cm (54 in); diameter 540 cm (18 ft)
Sussex £36,700 ($58,353)
20.V.97

Doulton produced a number of garden fountains and ornaments between 1870 and 1910, and George Tinworth was one of the medium's leading exponents, with his architectural effects proving highly successful. The centrepiece of this impressive piece is a shallow, scalloped bowl set on a fluted column, flanked by a pair of putti astride dolphins and a pair of swans. The surround, made up of a frieze of shells, is interrupted by six urns.

An Alabaster Relief of the Road to Calvary

?Middle Rhine, *c.* 1440, from the circle of the Master of the Lorch Calvary
18.9 × 29 cm (7½ × 11⅜ in)
London £28,750 ($47,438)
12.XII.96

Christ carrying the Cross is at the centre of this relief, surrounded by soldiers in contemporary armour. To the left is a standing figure of the Virgin with her hands clasped, and next to her stands St Veronica holding the vernicle. This relief is part of a much-discussed group of alabasters emanating from the Middle Rhine, but which take their

inspiration from the *Madonna dell'Acqua Pietà* in the church of San Francisco at Rimini. Although the artist is unknown, the inscription shows that he was of German origin, and, stylistically, the relief is close to a fired-clay group dated *c.* 1425 originally in the church of St Martin zu Lorch on the Rhine, south of Cologne.

An Ivory Group of the Virgin and Child

Second half of the 14th century
Height 21.5 cm (8½ in)
London £47,700 ($78,705)
12.XII.96

In this group the Christ Child sits upright in the Virgin's arms and holds an orb in his left hand, while playing with a dove's wing with his right. The figure is very similar in composition to one in the Germanisches National Museum, Munich, the origin of which was thought to be French or Rhenish. This particular figure is almost certainly from France, as the Virgin's oval face and almond eyes are more typical of French work of this period.

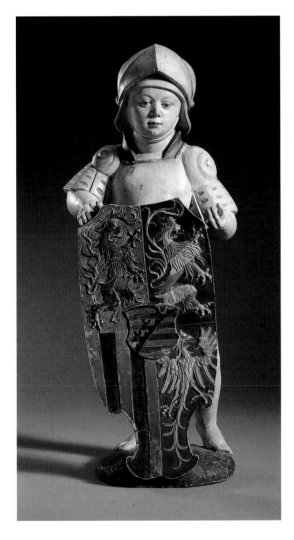

A Polychrome Stone Figure of an Heraldic Page
From a monument to the house of Saxony, mid-16th century, circle of Adoph Daucher
Height 50.2 cm (19¾ in)
London £17,250 ($28,635)
2.VII.97

It has been suggested that this figure comes from the Saxon Electoral Monument in Dresden, of which only the central panel survives. The monument was commissioned in 1553 by August, Elector Duke of Saxony, and the arms carried by this stone page are either those of his brother, who preceded him as Elector, or of their father. A watercolour of 1591 shows the complete monument, with heraldic pages at the top. Although these figures are naked, and the boy shown here is clothed in armour, the unclothed figures may be an artistic simplification.

A Polychrome and Limewood Group of the Virgin and Child
Swabia, first quarter of the 16th century, attributed to Jörg Lederer
Height 116 cm (45⅝ in)
London £52,100 ($86,484)
2.VII.97

The Virgin holds the Christ Child in her arms. Her veil flows over her red robe and blue and gold cloak, and she stands on a crescent moon. Certain aspects of the figure are characteristic of Jörg Lederer's work, in particular the drapery with its long, curving vertical fold and short, crisp 'v' folds. The figure bears similiarities to a sculpture of the Virgin in the former Kaiser-Friedrich Museum, Berlin, by Lederer, and the Tyrolean High Altar in the Heiligenblut Pfarrkirche by an unknown master, who was greatly influenced by Lederer.

Claude Michel, called Clodion
A Terracotta Group of the Crucifixion
French, c. 1785
Height 70 cm (27½ in)
London £52,100 ($84,315)
12.XII.96

This terracotta group is the only known surviving study for the crucifixion group that surmounted the roodscreen at Rouen Cathedral, which was destroyed during bombing in 1944. Clodion (1738–1814) was commissioned to sculpt the figure in 1777, and a model was produced in 1785. Changes were discussed, and the finished article was unveiled in 1788. From a photograph taken before the bombing it can be seen how the figure of Christ differs from the model, but because the Virgin and St John disappeared during the French Revolution, probably to be melted down, it is not possible to see how the whole compares.

Jean-Antoine Houdon
Bust of Benjamin Franklin
White marble, inscribed and
dated *F. P. Houdon en 1779*,
on reverse
Height with socle 53 cm
(20⅞ in)
New York $2,917,500
(£1,779,675) 5.XII.96
From the Collection formed
by the British Rail Pension
Fund

Benjamin Franklin was
America's minister to France
during most of the American
Revolution, and it was during
this time that Houdon
produced his busts of the
statesman. The first portrait
bust of 1778 is now in the
Metropolitan Museum of
Art. In this version, Franklin
appears to be slightly older
and it is likely that Houdon
had more time to render the
likeness. The attention to
detail, such as the
buttonholes in the jacket,
the eyes, modelling of the
cheeks, chin and jowls is of
exceptional quality.
Houdon's ability to depict
minutiae with such
naturalism, along with his
grasp of Franklin's public
personality, suggest that the
bust was commissioned by
an important patron.

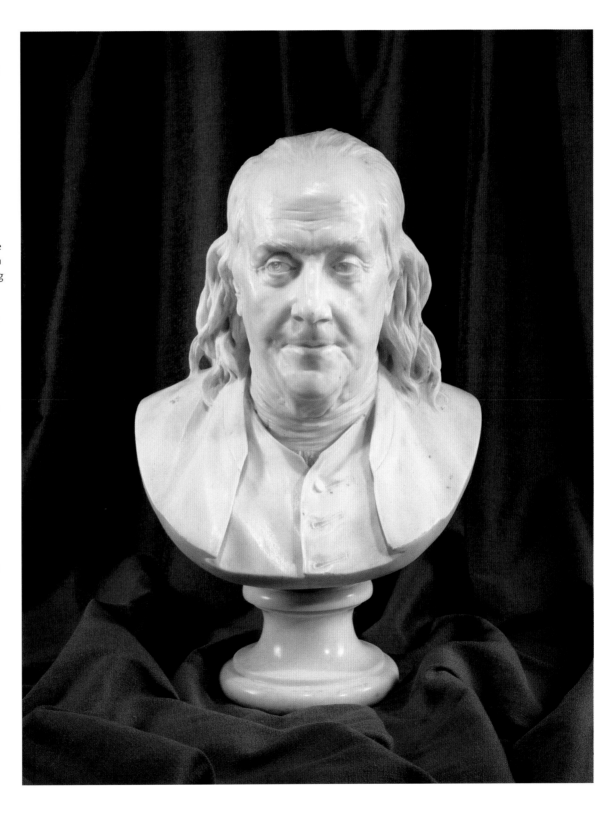

Jean-Léon Gérôme
Sarah Bernhardt
Patinated plaster, inscribed
J. L. GEROME and dedicated
À SARAH BERNHARDT
Height 67.9 cm (26¾ in)
New York $134,500 (£83,390)
23.V.97

Sarah Bernhardt's strength
of character, eccentricities of
behaviour and peculiarities
of taste made her famous
beyond her performances on
stage; she became an oft-
portrayed icon of her era.
This is the original plaster for
the polychromed marble
bust of the actress in the
collection of the Musée
d'Orsay, Paris. Having
carved the marble version in
1895, Gérôme painted this
plaster, inscribed it and gave
it to the actress.

Thomas Waldo Story
The Fallen Angel
Signed and dated *Waldo Story Roma 1887*
White marble on a stained wooden base, 76 × 188 cm (30 × 74 in)
London £128,000 ($208,640) 6.vi.97

This sculpture, exhibited in 1887, is a testament to the abiding influence on many sculptors of Antonio Canova's marble group *Cupid and Psyche*. However, despite these two groups being related compositionally, Story shifts the emotional balance of the protagonists, making the man's gesture full of tenderness, while the contorted languorousness of the angel is generations apart from Canova's neo-classical Psyche. The depiction of the figures is, as E. March Phillipps noted, 'entirely poetic in character'.

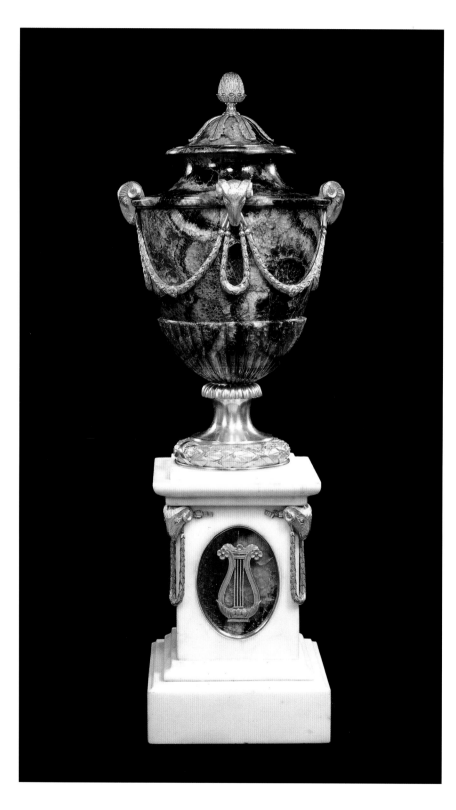

An Anglo-Russian Blue John and Gilt-Bronze-Mounted Vase

c. 1850–75, in the manner of Matthew Boulton

77 × 26 cm (2 ft 6 in × 10 in)

London £205,000 ($342,350)

15.xi.96

This magnificent vase is one of the largest of its kind ever recorded. The solid block of blue john was originally quarried in Derbyshire and the design of the vase is characteristic of the work of the great English manufacturer Matthew Boulton, a specialist in the production of this type of ormolu-mounted blue john vase. However, various features of construction and decoration suggest the involvement of foreign craftsmen and it is almost certain that the vase was produced in Russia, since the vase carries an inscription indicating provenance from the Russian Imperial collections at Peterhof, St Petersburg.

A George II Scarlet-Japanned Bureau Bookcase
c. 1725–50, in the manner of
Giles Grendey
Height 246 cm (8 ft 1 in),
width 113 cm (44½ in), depth
66 cm (26 in)
New York $420,500
(£257,640) 25.1.97

Giles Grendey (1693–1780)
was renowned for his quality
lacquered furniture produced
for the export trade. Bureau
bookcases lacquered in
scarlet were a particularly
important part of the large
trade in English furniture
made for the Spanish
market. The famous Lazcano
suite, which Grendey
supplied c. 1735–40 for the
Duke of Infantado's castle of
Lazcano in northern Spain,
had four bookcases of this
type, to which this piece can
be compared. It has black
and gold chinoiseries and
mirror-inset doors; below the
doors are two small slides to
hold candles.

A George II Brass-Mounted Inlaid Burl Walnut and Walnut Bureau Bookcase

c. 1730
Height 2.63 m (8 ft 7½ in); width 1.14 m (45 in); depth 64.8 cm (25½ in)
New York $310,500 (£186,300) 12.XII.96

An old paper label, apparently of eighteenth-century date and inscribed in Spanish, indicates that this bureau cabinet was once in a Spanish collection, having probably been made for export. Records of exports of English furniture to Spain show that bureau cabinets of this type were especially popular; the exuberant design, with gilt-metal serpents and female masks, closely reflects the tastes of Spanish collectors at this period.

A Rosewood Brass-Mounted and Brass-Inlaid Side Cabinet

c. 1815, attributed to George Bullock
Height 93 cm (3 ft ¼ in);
width 110 cm (3 ft 7 in); depth
67 cm (2 ft 2½ in)
London £126,900 ($213,192)
4.VII.97

This cabinet, first recorded in the collection of Queen Mary at Marlborough House, is securely attributed to the leading early-nineteenth-century cabinet-maker George Bullock. The cabinet is strikingly similar to a pair supplied by Bullock to the 4th Duke of Atholl for

Dunkeld, Perthshire in 1817–18, and was formerly sold through Sotheby's in 1969, entering the collection of the leading furniture historians, the late John and Helena Hayward.

**A Japanese Black Lacquer
and Gilt-bronze Commode
by François Linke**
Paris, *c.* 1910, after the model
by Joseph Baumhauer
90 × 147 cm (35⅜ × 57⅞ in)
London £78,500 ($127,955)
28.11.97

In contrast to the tradition of
reveneering existing lacquer
panels on to a carcass, this
commode was sent to Japan
by trans-Siberian railway for
decoration by the master
lacquer artist, Akatsuka
Jitoku. The bronzes
enclosing the panels are
based on Baumhauer's
eighteenth-century original
but, as befits the most
important ébéniste of the
time, Linke freely
reinterpreted the designs,
giving his version of the
commode a sinuous and
sensuous appearance.

OPPOSITE

**One of a Pair of Medici
Vases by La Compagnie des
Cristalleries de Baccarat**
Paris, *c.* 1910
Crystal and gilt-bronze,
height 82 cm (32¼ in)
London £36,700 ($57,619)
4.x.96
From the Archives de la
Manufacture de Baccarat

Nineteenth-century glass
manufacturers encountered
many setbacks in their
attempts to create a perfectly
transparent product that
could be engraved and cut,
imitating the naturally
occuring rock crystal.
However, by 1909 – when the
prototypes for these vases

were shown at the Exposition
Internationale in Nancy – the
exhibition's jury were able to
exclaim 'we are stunned by
the matchless mastery which
went into shaping and
decorating the crystal.'

A French Figural Regulator

c. 1900, signed *Glenerle &*
Charpentier/Fant le Brawges
39 Paris
Silvered and gilt-bronze,
height 2.57 m (8 ft 5 in)
New York $200,500
(£128,320) 11.IX.96
From the Burbridge
Foundation Collection

The standard of this striking
piece is formed as a Louis
XVI style pedestal, cast with
rams' heads and hung with
berried foliate swags. A
silvered, classically dressed
female figure, her form
accentuated by diaphanous
robes, curves gracefully
around the pedestal, reaching
towards a lyre form clock.

Hannah Cohoon
Shaker gift drawing:
Tree of Light or *Blazing Tree*
1845
Tempera with graphite
underdrawing and pen and
brown ink on woven paper,
40.6 × 53 cm (16 × 20⅞ in)
New York $299,500
(£178,290) 19.1.97

Gift drawings, the most
private art of the Shakers,
were meant to encourage
consecration to Shaker faith
and practice. This, one of the
best-known of the gift
drawings, demonstrates the
place Shaker drawings hold
in American folk art. Hannah
Cohoon stated that her

drawings were an attempt
to translate visions she had
seen into what can be
brought to paper, and it is
this that gives her work
its immediacy.

English Needlework Picture
Initialled *EP*, dated *1746*
Green, yellow, blue, red, grey,
pink, black and white wool
and silk on a linen ground
42.9 × 64.1 cm (16⅞ × 25¼ in)
New York $101,500
(£60,900) 19.i.97
The Joan Stephens Collection

This picture possibly depicts
the maker's family and their
home. Four of the nine
family members have died
and are shown lying in
draped and swagged tents.
Another very similar panel,
almost certainly worked by
the same hand, exists in a
private collection in
England, dated eight years
earlier. The same characters
are present in similar poses,
the only differences being
that in the 1738 piece there
are nine live members of the
family and one dead. The
existence of two such similar
domestic embroideries is
extremely rare.

**A Cigarstore Figure
of Punch**
c. 1850–75
Carved and painted pine,
180 cm (71 in)
New York $107,000
(£67,410) 19.x.96

This carved and painted
figure of the puppet-show
character Punch wears a
green peaked cap, a white
ruffled collar and a red-and-
green costume with gold
embellishments. In one hand
he holds a bunch of cigars
and with the other he points
back into the store outside
which he once stood. The
stepped rectangular base is
inscribed '*Cigars*' on the front,
and '*Tobacco*' on each side.

A Queen Anne Carved and Figured Mahogany Bonnet-Top Highboy
Goddard-Townsend School, Newport, Rhode Island, 1750–70
Height 2.18 m (7 ft 2 in), width 1.03 m (3 ft 4½ in), depth 52.1 cm (20½ in)
New York $910,000 (£541,720) 17.1.97

A masterpiece of American furniture, this highboy displays numerous details of construction and ornament that firmly tie it to the Goddard and Townsend craft tradition. Its overall understatement in design and ornament attest to the unique aesthetic sensibility of the conservative Quaker community on Easton's Point in Newport where the Goddard and Townsend School flourished from 1750 to 1800. The highboy's proportions are exceptional, as is the attention to detail.

A Queen Anne Carved Cherrywood Scalloped-Top Lowboy
Connecticut, c. 1770
Height 80.7 cm (31¾ in), width of top 91.4 cm (36 in), width of case 77.8 cm (30⅝ in), depth 53.7 cm (21⅛ in)
New York $387,500 (£228,625) 16.i.97
From the Collection of Mr and Mrs James O. Keene

The scalloped top on this rare lowboy embodies one of the most distinctive traits developed in the Connecticut Valley. There are at least thirty examples of scalloped-top pieces known, most of which are tied to the areas around Wethersfield, Connecticut, Hatfield, Northampton and Deerfield, Massachusetts. Cherry is almost always the primary wood used, often stained to resemble mahogany, with white pine as the secondary wood. This piece retains an old finish and a rich colour.

The Jacob Meyers Queen Anne Carved and Figured Walnut Open Armchair
Philadelphia, Pennsylvania, c. 1750
Height of seat 45.7 cm (18 in), height of crest 107 cm (42 in)
New York $519,500 (£316,895) 18.vi.97

This fine example of late Philadelphia Queen Anne style, which appears to retain its original, rich golden-brown finish, was originally the property of Jacob Meyers, who settled in Pennsylvania in the first half of the eighteenth century. The chair was given to his son, Jacob and thereafter passed through the family (now named Myers) to women named Margaret. A letter from the consignor states, '. . . the women in this family were NOT "shrinking violets." From just the lore that has passed down, they were very active in the family fortunes and were well educated.'

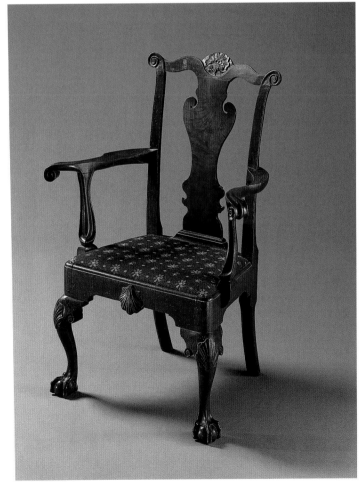

EUROPEAN TAPESTRIES

La Toilette
Attributed to the atelier of
François Picon, from a
sketch by François Boucher
Aubusson, c. 1760
242 × 477 cm (96¾ ×
190¾ in)
Zurich SF148,300 (£69,299;
$113,206) 10.XII.96

The original version of this
tapestry, which was one of six
in a series entitled *La Tenture
Chinoise*, was woven at
Beauvais from 1743. This
example comes from a later
weaving at Aubusson and
changes to the design can be
noted, particularly in the
addition of the group of three
children on the left, and the

standing girl. During the
Rococo period in eighteenth-
century Europe chinoiserie
became popular as a theme
for interior decoration,
fuelled by interest in
travellers' tales from the
Far East. The style was
based on rather fanciful
ideas about China, as
reflected in this tapestry.

A Bruges Allegorical Tapestry of the Apotheosis of the Seven Liberal Arts
After designs by Cornelis Schut, *c.* 1650–75
376 × 523 cm (12 ft 4 in × 17 ft 2 in)
New York $145,500
(£90,210) 31.1.97

This tapestry represents the last in a series of eight weavings of the Seven Liberal Arts after designs by Cornelis Schut (1597–1655). It is the only Bruges seventeenth-century series for which the artist of the designs is known. Three different border designs were employed for the series, and

this tapestry uses the second one. The tapestry depicts winged Astronomy, Music seated at an organ, Grammar holding a whip, Geometry with a terrestrial globe, Arithmetic at a table with a young man holding a book of numbers, Rhetoric and two men in discussion behind her representing Logic.

CONTINENTAL FURNITURE

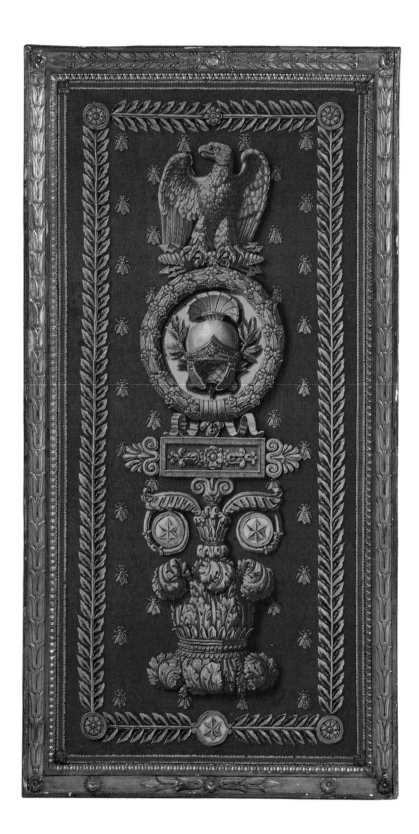

A Bureau Cabinet
Venetian, mid-18th century
Walnut, burr-walnut and
parcel-gilt, 296 × 170 ×
70 cm (9 ft 8½ × 5 ft 7 ×
2 ft 3½ in)
London £540,000
($896,400) 13.XII.96

Deriving its form from the
Anglo-Dutch repertory, the
bureau cabinet rapidly
became the most important
piece of furniture in the
palaces of the ancient
Venetian aristocracy and rich
merchants. The finest
examples, which are found in
the most important palaces of
the lagoon, were veneered in
burr walnut which was
highlighted with parcel-gilt
carved elements and
engraved mirrors, as on this
example. The presence of an
eagle on the cresting probably
refers to the coat of arms of
the family that originally
commissioned the cabinet.

**One of a Set of Six Gobelins
Tapestry Panels Made for
Napoleon I**
After the design of Saint-
Ange, in carved giltwood
frame, designed by Fontaine
and executed by Jacob-
Desmalter, ordered in 1807
and delivered in 1811
Height 136 cm (4 ft 5½ in),
width 70.5 cm (2 ft 3¾ in)
London £353,500 ($579,740)
13.VI.97

These panels (originally
mounted as a six-leaf screen)
were part of an important
suite of seat furniture
commissioned for the Grand
Cabinet of Napoleon I at the
Tuileries and supervised by
Percier and Fontaine,
Napoleon's official architects
and decorators. The suite
comprised of two large
ceremonial armchairs, six
armchairs, six chairs, twenty-
four stools, two footstools, a
screen and a firescreen,
covered in Gobelins tapestry
and mounted on carved
giltwood frames. The
designs for the tapisserie of
the entire suite were
completed by architect Saint-
Ange, while Fontaine
designed the frames, which
were then executed by Jacob-
Desmalter.

A Jewel Casket Made for William Beckford

c. 1792–1801

114 × 68.5 × 52 cm
(44¾ × 26⅞ × 20⅜ in)
Monaco FF5,292,500
(£555,713; $910,310) 14.VI.97

This jewel casket was identified thanks to a drawing by Jean-Guillaume Moitte (1746–1810) inscribed '*diamantaire de Lord Beckford*' and '*h. Auguste*'. The casket is the result of a collaboration between the sculptor and draughtsman Moitte and the silversmith Henri Auguste. Beckford had discovered the work of Auguste whilst in Madrid in 1787 and, between 1788 and 1802, commissioned four ewers from him, one in gold and three in silver. Moitte's rigorous neo-classical drawings provided the designs for at least three other pieces of furniture commissioned by Beckford.

A Louis XVI Bronze and Gilt-bronze Clock in a Bust of Minerva

1787, signed
Monaco FF3,540,500
(£410,698; $679,776)
14.XII.96

François-Louis Godon established himself in Paris *c.* 1764 but was involved in a wide range of activities before becoming the clockmaker of the Spanish Court. In 1784 he joined forces with the watchmaker Jean-Baptiste-André Furet to create the celebrated pendulum clock *à la négresse*, which was acquired in the same year by Louis XVI. This collaboration lasted until Godon's death, and Furet was named as the executor of Godon's will in 1802.

A Pair of Louis XV Ormolu Chenets

Second quarter 18th century, one signed on the base
*SOLON
54.6 × 43.2 cm (21½ × 17 in)
New York $574,500
(£350,445) 22.V.97

The variety and number of equine statues around Europe attest to the importance of the horse in the life of man. However, only rarely did purely decorative objects incorporating horses feature in Europe's great houses, ensuring that exceptions are almost always pieces of importance. These horses may have been inspired by the 'Marly Horses' by G. Coustou or were possibly modelled after the *Horses of Apollo* by Gaspard and Balthazard Marsy, which were originally intended for the Grotto of Thetis at Versailles.

A Louis XVI Bureau Plat
Ormolu-mounted ebony,
signed *E. Levasseur, JME*, late
18th century
76.8 × 163 × 80.7 cm
(30¼ × 64 × 31¾ in)
New York $398,500
(£243,085) 2.xi.96

The rectangular top of this
piece is inset with a gilt-
tooled leather writing surface
surrounded by a moulded
ormolu border. The frieze
has three drawers with
ormolu keyhole escutcheons
and borders. The bureau plat
is raised on circular, tapered,
ormolu-fluted legs inset with
chandelles ending in
campana-shaped feet.

CERAMICS AND GLASS

A Ralph Toft Slipware Charger

Inscribed *RALPH: TOFT 1676*
Diameter 43.5 to 44.8 cm
(17⅛ to 17⅝ in)
New York $85,000 (£53,550)
15.x.96

Very few dated slipware dishes by Ralph Toft, thought to be the brother of the better known Thomas Toft, have been recorded but those known seem to be dated primarily 1676 and 1677. This 'cavalier' dish features a central figure brandishing two swords above his head. The crowned heads on either side appear to derive from a similar motif used at the time on the arms of a number of the Stuart nobility.

**A Pair of Sèvres Porcelain
Ormolu-Mounted Écaille-
Ground Topographical
Vases**
Dated *1823*, views signed
Lebel
Heights overall 62.9 cm
(24¾ in) and 61.6 cm
(24¼ in)
New York $140,000
(£89,600) 11.ix.96
From the Burbridge
Foundation Collection

This pair of vases is a fine
example of the extraordinary
production of the Sèvres
factory under Alexandre
Brongniart who, as Director
from 1800 to 1847, brought a
new vibrance to French
porcelain at the beginning of
the Restoration by
continually searching for new
designs, techniques, colours,
sources and artists. Most
successful were vases such

as these, which combined
unusual colour grounds –
here the *écaille de tortue*
ground developed in
imitation of tortoiseshell –
with gilt borders framing
topographical views by
painters such as Nicolas-
Antoine Le Bel, whose
artistry is featured here.

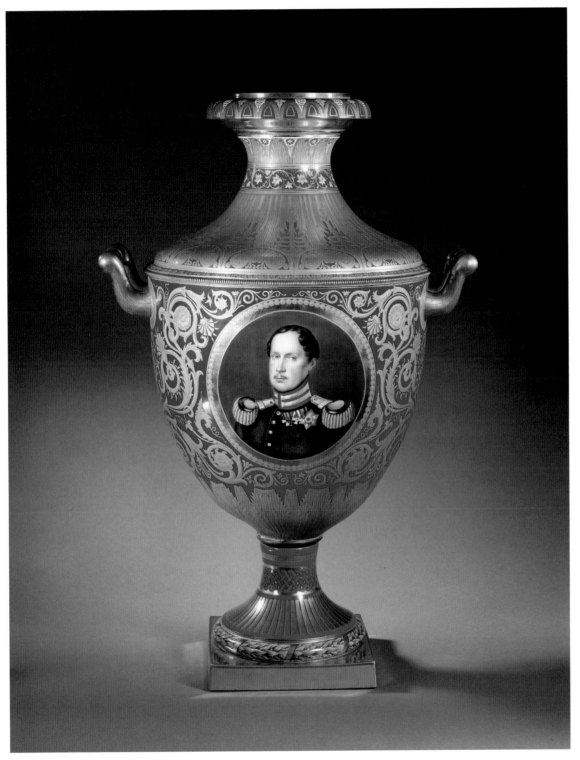

One of a Berlin Blue-ground Five-vase Garniture
c. 1834
Heights 78 cm (30¾ in),
61 cm (24 in) and 51 cm
(20 in)
London £309,500 ($523,055)
9.VII.97

The collection of Berlin
porcelain from which this
piece derives reflected the
city and its surroundings at a
time when it became one of
the most important and
beautiful capitals of Europe.
This garniture of five vases
was presented by King
Friedrich Wilhelm III of
Prussia to the General and
Minister of State, Graf von
Lottum. The central vase
(shown here) is painted with
a portrait of the king; the
other four pieces are
decorated with views of
Berlin and surrounding
areas, including the Neues
Palais and Sanssouci.

A Bohemian or South German Engraved Blue-cased Goblet and Cover
Attributed to Franz Paul Zach, *c.* 1860
Height 61 cm (24 in)
London £65,300 ($109,051)
19.XI.96

It is believed that this goblet was originally commissioned by a Russian tsar – possibly Alexander II – as a gift to his wife. Of outstanding quality, the decorative work on the piece suggests that it was conceived for a major international exhibition where it may have been chosen as a model for a tsarist gift. The blue overlay is finely cut through on one side to reveal the sleeping figure of Luna, the goddess of the moon, flanked by her winged daughter, Horae and a youth, and on the reverse shows an elaborate lion mask and scroll.

A Meissen Figure of a Lady of the 'Mopsorden'

Modelled by J. J. Kändler,
c. 1744
Height 27.5 cm (10⅞ in)
London £24,150 ($39,365)
17.VI.97

Frederick Augustus (the Strong), Elector of Saxony founded the Meissen porcelain factory in 1710. Figurines were a particular favourite of his and many masterpieces of the genre were produced during J. J. Kändler's time at Meissen, 1731–75. This example is traditionally said to represent the Elector's favourite mistress, Gräfin Kosel.

A Minton Majolica Cistern

Dated *1873*, impressed
MINTONS, with a fitted metal liner
Length 95.3 cm (37½ in)
New York $50,600 (£31,625)
11.III.97

Described by Minton as a 'cistern', this piece actually was intended to be used as a wine-cooler. Decorated in the Renaissance style, at each end stands a putto, one symbolizing Summer, the other Autumn. Both figures wear wreaths and carry bouquets fashioned from the bounty of their seasons: wheat and poppies or grape-laden vines.

APPLIED ART

A Daum Nancy Internally Decorated and Applied Glass Vase
1905–10, inscribed
Daum/Nancy with croix de Lorraine
39.4 cm (15½ in)
New York $98,750 (£60,237)
11.VI.97

Made of grey glass and shaped like a gourd, this vase is internally streaked with mustard yellow and its surface is richly embellished with mottled applied coloured glass powders in shades of crimson, orange, turquoise and forest green. The textures and colours simulate rust and mould on an over-ripe gourd. The handle – the gourd's stem – is striped in yellow and green and trails about the body of the vase.

A Tiffany Favrile Glass and Bronze Lotus Lamp on a Mosaic Lily-Pad Base
c. 1900
Height 88.3 cm (34¾ in), diameter 71.1 cm (28 in)
New York $1,102,500 (£674,310) 7.XII.96

This lamp ties with the Virginia Creeper lamp for the highest price achieved for a piece by Tiffany. There were only three examples of the Lotus lamp made, selling for $750 each at a time when a six-bedroom house could be bought for $1,000. Electricity was a recent invention when this lamp was designed, but Tiffany had already been working with the new invention for twenty years, on occasion in collaboration with its inventor, Thomas Edison.

**Emile-Jacques Ruhlmann
A Sèvres Porcelain and
Silvered-bronze Lamp**
Enamelled mark *s/1927/DN*
MADE IN FRANCE
Height 193 cm (6 ft 4 in)
New York $96,000 (£58,560)
11.VI.97

This beautifully plain lamp is
one of six designed by
Ruhlmann for the first-class
salon of the ocean liner
Île-de-France; only two
survive. The illuminated
upper section in milky white
porcelain is raised on a
silvered-bronze scrolled
base, and sits on a
reproduction plinth in
Porter marble.

**Christian Dell at the
Metallwerkstatt Bauhaus
Weimar
Wine Jug and Cover**
1922, designer/maker's
monogram 'CD'
Alpaca with hammered finish
and ebony, 20 cm (7⅞ in)
London £100,500 ($163,815)
1.XI.96
From the Torsten Bröhan
Collection

This jug is a landmark piece
in the history of design at the
Bauhaus. It is earlier than
any other recorded example
of the fully elaborated
geometric constructions that
have come to be associated
with the school, principally
through the work of Christian
Dell and Marianne Brandt. It
was made for the christening
of Dell's nephew.

Louis Majorelle
A Two-tier Table
c. 1900
Burr thuya wood and
mahogany with gilt bronze,
height 81.25 cm (22 in),
maximum width 71 cm
(28 in)
London £38,900 ($63,407)
27.III.97

The muscular, bowed legs of
this table support a shaped
top with a carved surround
and, with buttress supports,
enclose a waisted lower
shelf. Gilt-bronze mounts
add a decorative element to
the table and highlight the
gentle curve of its legs and
top. Cast as stylized flowers
and leaves, the mounts run
down to foliate sabots.

Emile Gallé
A 'Rose de France' Vase
c. 1900, elaborate engraved
mark '*Gallé*'
21 cm (8¼ in)
London £93,900 ($153,057)
1.XI.96
From the Michael Caine
Collection

The clear glass of this vase
has been internally mottled
with pale green and rich
turquoise, and overlaid with
bubble-gum pink. It is carved
with delicate, fern-like fronds
against a partially textured
ground, and three rose buds
with stems and leaves – all
with naturalistically carved
details – have been applied.

PRECIOUS OBJECTS

JEWELLERY

An Invisibly Set Ruby and Diamond Flower Brooch
Aletto Brothers
New York $299,500
(£182,695) 7.IV.97

This seven-petalled flowerhead is invisibly set with calibré-cut rubies, framing a central cluster of round diamonds mounted *en tremblant*, weighing approximately 4.30 carats. A detachable stem (not illustrated) of baguette diamonds weighing approximately 4.00 carats accompanies the flowerhead, and the whole is set in platinum and 18 carat gold.

A Diamond Brooch
Black, Starr & Frost, signed, c. 1900
New York $90,500 (£55,205) 7.IV.97
Property formerly from the Estate of Marguerite Singer Wilson

Black, Starr & Frost was founded in the USA in 1810 and was known as the 'Diamond Palace of Broadway'. The company went on to create some of America's finest Art Deco jewellery. A 6.79 carat marquise-shaped diamond is at the centre of this brooch, surrounded by laurel wreaths and berries. Suspended from the sides of the brooch is a flexible garland of diamond-set leaves anchored by a pear-shaped diamond.

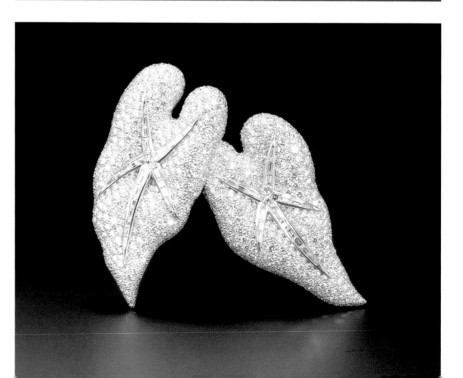

A Diamond Lillum Leaf Brooch
Herz-Belperron, France, signed
New York $68,500 (£41,785) 7.IV.97

The two joined leaves of this brooch are pavé-set with 709 round diamonds and decorated with star-shaped motifs of baguette diamonds mounted in platinum. Suzanne Belperron began her career in 1923 as a jewellery designer for René Boivin, and went on to work for Bernard Herz in 1933. With Herz's son Jean she formed Herz-Belperron, making jewellery that mixed colours and materials seldom before used in designs of abstracted natural forms. Once popular with royalty and stars of the entertainment world, Belperron's work suffered years of relative obscurity until a sale of jewellery belonging to the Duchess of Windsor at Sotheby's in 1987 caused a resurgence of interest in her designs.

A Sapphire and Diamond Ring
French
St Moritz SF773,500
(£327,191; $529,847) 22.11.97

The step-cut sapphire at the centre of this ring weighs 14.65 carats, is mounted in platinum and flanked by two baguette-cut diamonds. The accompanying Gübelin report states that the sapphire is of Kashmiri

origin. Kashmiri sapphires are among the world's rarest and most expensive gemstones, and come from mines 5,000 metres up in the Himalayas. Due to heavy snowfalls, the mines can only be accessed for two months during the summer. The sapphires are of an intense colour, described as 'cornflower blue', and look even more vivid in evening light.

A Ruby and Diamond Ring
Second half of the 19th century
St Moritz SF894,500
(£386,424; $612,733) 22.11.97

This oval-shaped Burmese ruby weighs 8.71 carats and is mounted within a border of cushion-shaped diamonds. The mount and shoulders are pierced and carved with scrolling tendrils and trefoils. Umberto II of

Italy gave this ring to his future wife, Princess Maria Josée of Belgium, later Queen Maria Josée of Italy, whom he married in 1930.

A Fancy Vivid Yellow Diamond Ring
New York $3,302,500
(£2,014,525) 7.IV.97
Property from the Estate of Julie V. Burden

This marquise-shaped fancy vivid yellow diamond weighs 13.83 carats, and is flanked by elongated baguette diamonds. There are additional small round diamonds around the bezel and on the prongs, and the whole is mounted in platinum.

A Natural 'Peacock' Colour Cultured Pearl Necklace
Length 43.18 cm (17 in)
New York $239,000
(£145,790) 7.IV.97

A single strand of thirty-three natural black-coloured pearls of 'peacock' hue are completed by a platinum ball clasp pavé-set with round diamonds. Black pearls are produced by the black-lipped oyster native to the waters of French Polynesia. 'Peacock' is the rarest colour the oysters produce, and the pearls of this necklace are also particularly large and of fine quality. Black pearls are in fact grey or bronze, and are sometimes naturally enhanced by silvery hues such as peacock, green or blue.

A Diamond Necklace

c. 1830
Length 47.5 cm (18⅝ in)
London £26,450 ($43,378)
19.VI.97

The openwork oval links of
this necklace are set with
cushion-shaped stones, each
with a large similarly cut
stone mounted at its centre
between diamond scrolled
motifs. Between each oval
link are cushion-shaped
diamond foliate motifs. The
necklace can also be worn as
a choker.

A Diamond 'Giardinetto' Brooch

c. 1920
London £47,700 ($78,228)
19.VI.97

Designed as a vase of
flowers, this brooch is set
with a large pear-shaped
stone and smaller rose and
cushion-shaped diamonds,
some of yellow tint. It was
sold with a fitted case by the
Goldsmiths and Silversmiths
Company.

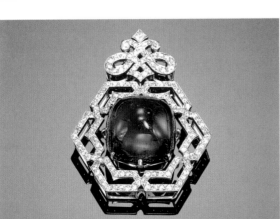

A Coloured Diamond Pendant

French, c. 1905
Geneva SF1,983,500
(£936,212; $1,561,015)
20.XI.96

The surmount of this piece is
collet-set with a kite-shaped
Fancy Blue diamond weighing
1.60 carats within a border of
millegrain-set cushion-
shaped diamonds. Below this
hangs a pear-shaped Fancy
Intense Blue diamond
weighing 3.98 carats on a
diamond box-set chain,
mounted on a necklet chain.

A Fancy Intense Blue Diamond Ring

Geneva SF3,083,500
(£1,341,323; $2,235,538)
21.V.97

This internally flawless, pear-
shaped Fancy Intense Blue
diamond weighs 5.07 carats
and is framed by nine
marquise-shaped diamonds.
The shoulders are accented
by pear-shaped stones
mounted in platinum.

A Fancy Vivid Purplish Pink Diamond Ring

Geneva SF1,763,500
(£767,123; $1,278,538)
21.V.97

Pear-shaped diamonds
surround the claw-set Fancy
Vivid Purplish Pink brilliant-
cut diamond, which weighs
2.15 carats and is extremely
rare. A letter from the GIA
accompanying the ring
states that the central
diamond is the largest of its
kind ever graded by the GIA.

A Cabochon Emerald and Diamond Pendant
Tiffany & Co., c. 1920, signed
New York $71,250 (£43,676)
11.VI.97
Property from an Ohio family

A sugarloaf cabochon
emerald weighing
approximately 30.00 carats is
flexibly set within an
openwork hexagonal frame
set with small, old European-

cut diamonds. A knot-design
pendant loop is used to
attach the pendant to a
delicate platinum chain. The
pendant was sold with a fitted
box stamped Tiffany & Co.

A Sapphire, Diamond and Pearl Parure

Bapst, c. 1863
Geneva SF1,378,500
(£599,648; $999,413) 21.v.97
Property of the Comte and
Comtesse de Paris

This parure was made from different pieces of jewellery, the property of Marie-Amélie, Queen of the French, and remounted for her by Bapst, the Royal Parisian Jewellers, in the second half of the nineteenth century. The queen bequeathed the parure to her youngest son, the Duc de Montpensier, having given her eldest grandson, the Comte de Paris, a similar parure. Ironically, the marriage of the Comte de Paris to the daughter of the Duc de Montpensier reunited both parures. This group is comprised of a tiara, a corsage ornament, a pair of epaulette brooches, a pair of matching earrings, the centre plaque of a bracelet and the original fitted red leather case by Bapst.

OPPOSITE

A Sapphire and Diamond Necklace

Late 19th century
Length 57.2 cm (22½ in)
New York $2,752,500
(£1,734,075) 22.x.96

This necklace originally belonged to Mary Scott Townsend, the daughter of William Lawrence Scott, a coal and railway magnate and a prominent citizen of Erie, Pennsylvania. In a portrait painted in 1894 Mary is shown wearing part of the necklace. Remodelled as it passed down through the generations of the family, this piece includes fifteen rare Kashmir sapphires, a gem that possesses an intense blue colour softened by a velvety textural appearance.

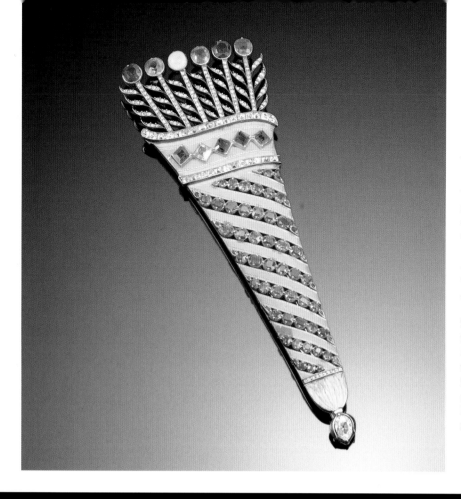

A Gold, Diamond and Gem-set Acrostic Brooch

Early 19th century
London £25,300 ($41,492)
19.VI.97

This brooch is designed as six arrows in a quiver; they terminate in, respectively, a garnet, an emerald, an opal, a ruby, a garnet and an emerald, spelling GEORGE. Published and illustrated in *Le XIXe Siècle Français, Collection Connaissance des Arts*, Edition Hachette, 1957 (p. 155, fig. 1), it was believed to have been given to the famous French comedienne Mlle George by Napoleon, whose mistress she was from 1803. After this they remained good friends, Mlle George offering to accompany him in his exile.

A Diamond Tiara in the Garland Style

Cartier, New York
c. 1920, signed
Geneva SF498,500
(£216,848; $361,413) 21.V.97

This tiara, made to special order, is designed as five graduating laurel wreaths each set at the centre with a circular-cut diamond drop. Four of the larger diamonds may be mounted as pendant earrings with the platinum fittings provided. The tiara is accompanied by a certificate of authority from Cartier and its original fitted blue leather case.

**A Ruby, Emerald, Sapphire
and Diamond Bracelet**
Cartier
Paris, *c.* 1930, signed *Cartier*
Length 18 cm (7 in)
Geneva SF432,500 (£188,138;
$313,563) 21.v.97

This bracelet is designed as
an embroidered ribbon and is
mounted in platinum. The
articulated links are
decorated with octagonal
motifs of calibré-cut rubies,
emeralds and sapphires,
each collet-set at the core
with a circular-cut sapphire.
The centre of the bracelet has
a step-cut sapphire enhanced
by enamel beads on a pavé-
set diamond ground.

A Set of Aquamarine and Diamond Jewels

Russian c. 1900, necklace length 35.5 cm (14 in), bracelet length 17.5 cm (6⅞ in)
London £73,000 ($114,610)
10.x.96

Imperial Jewels from the Collection of Princess Dorothea of Hesse

This diamond and aquamarine parure consists of a tiara, a necklace by Fabergé, a bracelet, probably by Fabergé, and a pair of earrings (not illustrated). These jewels once belonged to the Grand Duchess Elizabeth Feodorovna of Russia (1864–1918), who married Sergei Alexandrovitch, Grand Duke of Russia and son of Alexander II, Emperor of Russia. She was said to be stunningly beautiful and was showered with jewels by her husband. After her husband's assassination in 1905 she became the abbess of a convent, giving her jewels to members of her family.

A Natural Pearl Necklace
1919–29
Length 55.9 cm (22 in)
New York $464,500
(£292,635) 22.x.97

This necklace of sixty-three natural pearls with a diamond clasp was made by jeweller Raymond C. Yard. Yard's small business, which he started in 1922, had a select following – this piece was purchased by John D.

Rockefeller. The necklace took ten years to assemble, as Yard had to find – from the thousands of pearls harvested in that time – perfectly rounded specimens that graduated in proportion.

MINIATURES AND VERTU

OPPOSITE

**The 'Apple Blossom'
Fabergé Easter Egg**
St Petersburg
Nephrite with jewelled three-
colour gold and enamelled
silver mounts, workmaster
M. Perchin, engraved in
cyrillic *FABERGÉ 1901*, width
14 cm (5½ in)
Geneva SF1,300,000
(£613,207; $1,024,056)
19.XI.96

Following Imperial
precedent, this Easter Egg
was made for industrialist
and mining entrepreneur
Alexander Ferdinandovich
Kelch as a gift for his wife,
Barbara Petrovna.
Commissioned annually, the
series of seven ended when
the couple separated in
1904. The largest group of
such works made for anyone

outside the Imperial family,
their richness and delicacy
makes them equal to the
Imperial Eggs. The design of
the 'Apple Blossom' Egg
reflects the fashionable taste
for *style japonaise* and the
spirited rendering of sap-
filled spring boughs
becomes a metaphor for the
creativity that engendered it.

**A Hardstone Appliqué
Snuff Box**
Berlin, *c.* 1755–65
Four-colour gold mounts
and jewelled thumbpiece,
maker's mark of Daniel
Baudesson, width
8.2 cm (3¼ in)
Geneva SF399,500
(£171,785; $279,650) 20.V.97

Daniel Baudesson, court
jeweller to Frederick II, King
of Prussia (Frederick the
Great), is recorded as having
supplied eighteen snuff
boxes to the king between
1747 and 1765. The richly
assertive, almost three-
dimensional use of foiled
diamonds and other
gemstones in this example
is a characteristic of snuff
boxes commissioned by the
king. The subtly coloured
chinoiserie subjects, after
Boucher, reflect the king's
fascination with the Far East.

A Gold Self-Winding Minute Repeating Perpetual Calendar Wristwatch with Moon Phases

c. 1991, Cartier 'Pasha' no. 73
Diameter 3.8 cm (1½ in)
Hong Kong HK$515,000
(£41,200; $66,950) 1.v.97

Making watches since 1853, Cartier are most famous for their classic 'Tank' design wristwatch, first developed in 1917 and still in production today. As a result of collaboration with watch movement designers, Cartier have always produced complicated, innovative watches of which this is a good example.

A Platinum and Gold Cushion Minute Repeating Wristwatch

c. 1925, Patek Philippe & Co.,
signed, no. 138147
3.8 × 3 cm (1½ × 1⅛ in)
New York $662,500
(£410,750) 28.x.96

This piece is accompanied by a certificate from Patek Philippe confirming the manufacture of the movement in 1908 and subsequent sale of the watch in 1926. Originally intended as a lady's watch, it was finished in its present form by Patek Philippe in 1925 and sold to Tiffany's, where it was bought in 1926. Since then it has remained in the family of the original owner. This marks the first appearance at auction of a platinum and gold Patek Philippe minute repeating wristwatch.

A Stainless Steel Perpetual Calendar Wristwatch with Indirect Centre Seconds and Moon Phases

1944, Patek Philippe, signed
Diameter 3.5 cm (1⅜ in)
London £573,500 ($900,395)
3.x.96

Produced by the maker holding the world record prices for wristwatches sold at auction, this watch holds the record for the sale of a stainless steel wristwatch. It is unusual for having a complicated movement in a non-precious metal case. The indirect centre seconds mechanism (normally found in chronographs) was added to enable the second hand to be temporarily disengaged for accurate time setting. It later transpired that the mechanism made the watch lose time if triggered inadvertently and so was left dormant in the movement.

An Ebony Quarter Repeating Table Clock

William III *c.* 1700, Thomas
Tompion no. 377
Height 42 cm (16½ in)
London £85,100 ($142,117)
18. XII.96

The quarter repeating system was designed to meet the demand for a clock that could be used to tell the time at night or in poor light as well as during the day. Usually fitted with handles, the clock was meant to be carried to the bedroom at night. There were a variety of repeating systems made, but by far the most successful and accurate was invented by Thomas Tompion. This clock is fitted with such a mechanism: if the string is pulled the clock will strike the preceding hour followed by up to three blows on a separate bell to indicate which quarter has been passed.

A Mulberrywood Month Going Longcase Clock

William III, *c.* 1695, Thomas
Tompion no. 266
Height 206.5 cm (6 ft 9¼ in)
London £111,500 ($175,055)
3.X.96

Thomas Tompion, the most highly respected English clockmaker, was born in Bedfordshire in 1639. He moved to London and became a Free Brother of the Clockmakers' Company in 1671. Between 1680 and 1685, Tompion introduced a numbering system for his clocks and watches which makes it possible to date this clock, number 266, to around the time his apprentice, Edward Banger, was Freed in 1695. Banger later went into partnership with Tompion and after 1701 most clocks were signed with both names.

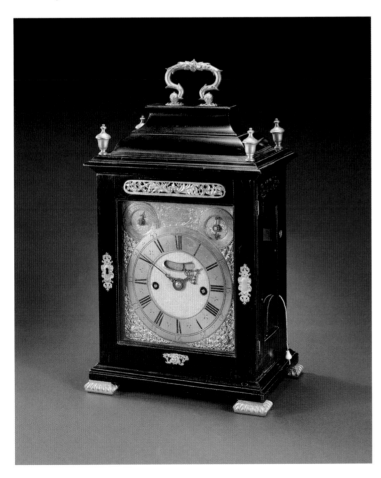

A Gold and Enamel Pair Cased Half Quarter Repeating Cylinder Watch

1756, Andrew Dickie, Edinburgh, no. 2045, signed
Diameter 5 cm (2 in)
London £65,300 ($109,051)
18.XII.96

Recognized as a fine maker of horological items, in 1761, Andrew Dickie was appointed as adviser to Parliament to study the clock made by John Harrison in response to the national project seeking a method for ships to measure longitude. This cylinder watch is outstanding, not for its movement, however, but for the vibrant and detailed classical scene on the outside case which is believed to be by the best enameller of his time, George Michael Moser.

A Gilt-Metal and Enamel Double-Dialled Heliocentric Astronomical Watch

c. 1785, attributed to Jacob Auch
Diameter 5.9 cm (2⅜ in)
Geneva SF176,500 (£69,146; $115,296) 19.XI.96

This rare example of a German astronomical watch has a white enamelled dial with four subsidiary dials, and on the reverse a planetarium on a revolving enamelled blue disc. At the centre of the planetarium is the sun, and the earth and its moon are shown, as well as signs of the zodiac, Mercury and Venus. The watch has a gilt cylinder movement with large balance, and is stored in a custom-built fitted leather box.

A Heavy Gold Hunter Cased Tourbillon Minute Repeating Split Second Chronograph Watch with Perpetual Calendar, Moon Phases and Register

1900, S. Smith & Son, no. 1900–1, signed; the movement by Nicole, Nielsen & Co.
Diameter 5.9 cm (2⅜ in)
New York $145,500 (£90,210) 28.X.96

S. Smith & Son were makers to the Admiralty of watches accurate enough to be recognized by the Royal Observatory at Kew. The number of this watch suggests that it was the first of its series to be manufactured in 1900 and may in fact be the first watch produced by the company in the twentieth century. An already complex mechanism is enhanced by the tourbillon carriage, only included in watches made by the master watchmakers.

A Gold, Enamel and Split-Pearl Jump Seconds Quarter Repeating Musical Automaton Watch with Concealed Erotic Scene

c. 1820, Piguet & Meylan
Diameter 5.3 cm (2⅛ in)
Geneva SF295,000
(£126,555; $207,680) 20.v.97

The variety of special features in this watch suggest that it was made to order. A combination of automaton, repeat and music as well as a high-quality enamel case are unusual, but the addition of a concealed erotic scene make this almost certainly the prized possession of a wealthy and discerning patron. The enamel work on the panels is unsigned and though this was not unusual for artists working in Geneva in the early nineteenth century, the style of the painting on this watch indicates a hand that was closest to Jean François Dupont (1785–1863).

A Gold, Enamel, Pearl and Turquoise Openface Quarter Repeating Musical Centre Seconds Watch

c. 1810
Diameter 5.4 cm (2⅛ in)
New York $147,700
(£90,097) 11.11.97

This is an example of the style of watch produced to meet the demand created by the enormous trade between Peking and the West in the late eighteenth and early nineteenth centuries. Buyers in the Orient favoured highly decorative cases, such as this polychrome guilloche enamel, and complicated mechanisms, demonstrated here with the addition of music to the quarter repeating feature.

A Pair of Louis XV Royal Silver Wine Coolers
Claude Ballin II, Paris, 1744–45
Height 25.4 cm (10 in)
New York $3,962,500
(£2,417,1,25) 13.XI.96
The property of George Ortiz

These wine coolers were traditionally attributed to Thomas Germain but careful scrutiny of the unclear maker's mark reveals the initials CB for Ballin. They form part of the composite Penthièvre-Orléans service

and miraculously survived melting to finance Louis XV's wars and again during the Revolution when, although seized, the service was spared on account of its quality.

A Dutch Silver Coffee Pot and Hot Milk Jug
Servatius Beckers,
Maastricht, 1774–75
Height of coffee pot 29.7 cm
(11⅝ in)
Amsterdam Dfl123,900
(£39,400; $65,171) 26.v.97

This matching coffee pot and milk jug have scrolled wood handles and acorn and leaf finials. The spouts are chased with fish heads and bulrushes. The coat of arms is that of Scherpenzeel (de) Heusch of 's Hertogenbosch.

A Silver Pot-à-oille, Cover, Liner and Stand
Charles Spire, Paris, 1752–53
Height 34 cm (13⅜ in)
Monaco FF2,982,500
(£313,163; $515,990) 15.vi.97

The pot-à-oille is the French term for a circular tureen in which a highly spiced ragout or *olla* was served. This dish, of Spanish origin, was made fashionable by Queen Marie-Thérèse, the wife of Louis XIV. This example was commissioned from the Parisian silversmith Charles Spire by Dom Francisco da Silva Telo e Meneses, 1st Marquês de Vagos

(1723–1808) whose arms appear on the cover, liner and stand. It follows the fashion set by the Portuguese royal family who, enriched at the beginning of the eighteenth century by the wealth of Brazil's silver and gold mines, turned to France for the finest silver. Thus began the Portuguese love affair with French silver.

A George III Silver-Gilt Almoner's Dish
Thomas Heming, London, 1761
Diameter 64 cm (25 in)
London £63,100 ($103,484)
5.VI.97
From the Collections of the Earls of Warwick

At a coronation the High Almoner distributed the blue cloth on which the sovereign walked in Westminster Hall. For this he was traditionally rewarded with an Almoner's dish. At the coronation of George III the Earl of Exeter was appointed to carry out these duties and should have been awarded 'two large chased basons' for his services. George III chose to withhold the dish illustrated here and later presented it to his goddaughter, Lady Georgiana Murray Greville, as a christening gift in 1798.

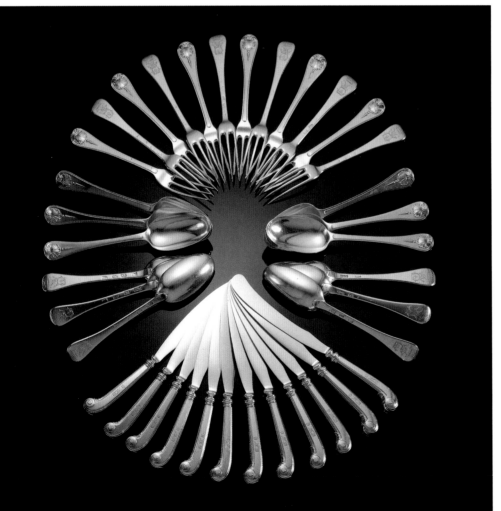

A George I and George II Silver Dessert Service
Joseph Barbutt, London, c. 1726–31
London £34,500 ($56,580)
5.VI.97

These twelve knives, twelve spoons and twelve forks come in a shagreen case with brass handles and lock. It is engraved with a crest below a viscount's coronet and has a Hanoverian thread shell and drop pattern and is the earliest English example known in this form.

The Emlen Salver
Richard Humphreys,
Philadelphia, c. 1775
Diameter 41.9 cm (16½ in)
New York $250,000
(£147,500) 16.1.97

This salver was commissioned by George Emlen IV, a member of the wealthy landowning Emlen family who first arrived in Philadelphia in 1682. At the centre of the salver is his monogram, GE. Emlen ordered a number of items in silver from Humphreys, most of which are now in the Philadelphia Museum of Art. A Quaker, Humphreys was born in the West Indies and became well known as a fine silversmith through a commission to make the Charles Thomson tea urn in 1774. The urn, ordered by the Continental Congress as a gift for the secretary, is the largest and rarest holloware form in eighteenth-century American silver.

A Pair of German Parcel-Gilt Globe Cups

Andreas Bergmann
(Berckmann), Nuremberg,
c. 1655
Height 22.9 cm (9 in)
New York $585,500
(£368,865) 16.x.96

One of these cups is engraved with the map of the world and the other with a plan of the heavens, as known in the early seventeenth century. The former is supported by the figure of Caesar. A Latin inscription under the base reads '. . . I first emperor . . . deserve this world of ours [which] rests upon my shoulders'. The celestial cup is supported by the kneeling figure of Hercules, wearing a lion's pelt, with his knee resting on his club. The inscription in this instance reads: 'The educated mind is hardly born to rest on earth. It goes on high . . .'

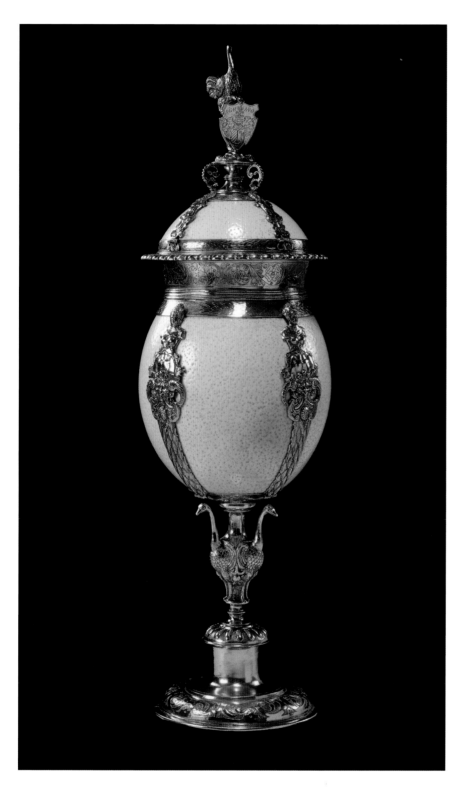

A German Silver-Gilt Mounted Ostrich Egg Cup and Cover

Andreas Klette, Torgau,
c. 1622
Height 45 cm (17⅝ in)
Geneva SF663,500
(£285,968; $467,104) 19.v.97

The stem of this cup takes the form of three ostriches, and an ostrich finial stands above the shield on the cover. The initials and armorials on the shield are those of Hans Adam von der Osten. The cup was given to him by his wife Eva on the tenth anniversary of their wedding and the fortieth anniversary of his birth. She chose the ostrich egg as a pun on her maiden name, von Straussen.

A Wanli Porcelain 'Crowcup' with German Parcel-Gilt Silver Mounts

Peter Wiber(s),
Nuremberg, c. 1610
Height 17 cm (6⅝ in)
Geneva SF212,500 (£91,587;
$149,600) 19.v.97

Dating from the Wanli period (1573–1619), this Chinese bowl is made of 'Kraak' porcelain. The word was coined by the Dutch after the Portuguese carracks that carried the porcelain cargoes from China. Kraak porcelain was not known in any quantity in western Europe until the beginning of the seventeenth century when the Dutch captured two Portuguese carracks in 1602 and 1604. The sale of the cargoes by auction caused a sensation, as the porcelain was obviously of higher quality than the French- and Italian-made pottery used at the time.

COLLECTORS' SALES

STAMPS

Southern Rhodesia 1931, 'Victoria Falls' 3d
Waterlow and Sons artist's original watercolour artwork
London £4,600 ($7,636)
13.XII.96

The original watercolour artwork for this stamp was executed in shades of blue and Chinese white. It was produced by a house artist at Waterlow and Sons in England and has the seal of the High Commissioner for Southern Rhodesia on the reverse.

South West Africa 1931, Pictorial Issue
Hand-painted composite essay sunk in a presentation card
Johannesburg R143,000 (£19,070; $31,780) for set of twelve values 25.VI.97

This is one of a unique set of twelve hand-painted essays produced by an artist at Bradbury Wilkinson & Co. Ltd in England. This 20-shilling value is a fine depiction of the Okuwahaken Falls. There are 'approval' cachets of the Director of Posts and Telegraphs at Windhoek on the reverse.

China 1897, Chungking Local Post 2 Candarins Postcard from Chungking to England
Hong Kong HK$115,000 (£9,090; $14,877) 7.XI.96

This pictorial postal card of the Chungking Local Post was sent from Chungking to England via the Imperial Chinese Post Office. It was carried to Shanghai and there passed to the French Post Office for onwards transmission to London. Local Post stamps and postal stationery had no validity outside the Local Post system – hence the use of other adhesive stamps to pay the prevailing postage rates.

China 1877, Series of Designs by De La Rue for the Proposed First Issue of Chinese Postage Stamps
Hong Kong HK$1,670,000 (£132,855; $216,041) 15.v.97

This unique series of hand-painted essays were produced by De La Rue for the proposed first issue of Chinese postage stamps. The designs had been submitted in response to an enquiry from the London representative of Chinese customs. They are a unique combination of the very finest work produced by De La Rue's artisans, coupled with an almost overpowering influence of the best in Chinese iconography, unseen in any other work produced by De La Rue up to that time. These designs were passed over in favour of a locally designed stamp that features a rather friendly dragon as the central motif.

United States of America, Roosevelt Small Die Proof Album, 1847–1902
New York $47,150 (£28,290) 27.xi.96

This album contains 308 small die proofs mounted on gilt-edged thick grey cards in a leather binder, inscribed 'John Kay'. This was one of eighty-five albums prepared for distribution in 1903, and is one of the few to survive intact. The album is accompanied by a letter to John Kay from Edward C. Madden, Third Assistant Postmaster General, which helped to date the albums correctly, and describes how it was Madden's idea to have 'a few extra sets of the proofs struck off for distribution to some friends'.

Since January 1997 all Sotheby's Postage Stamp sales in Asia have been held in association with Corinphila of Zurich

Ultra-High Relief Double Eagle
United States of America, 1907, Roman Numerals, designed by Augustus Saint-Gaudens
New York $825,000 (£495,000) 16.XII.96

In 1905 Augustus Saint-Gaudens was commissioned by President Theodore Roosevelt to produce a coinage not only aesthetically worthy of the ancients but also imitative of their sculptural use of relief. Rising to the challenge, the artist designed a coin the monumentality and grandeur of which successfully convey his intention to 'make it a living thing'. Due to this version's highly sculptural relief, it proved impossible to mass-produce and few (up to twenty-four struck with two being melted) are extant. This coin, the Bloomfield specimen, achieved a world record for any gold coin sold at auction.

Indian Mutiny Victoria Cross Group, awarded to Lieutenant-Colonel T. B. Hackett, Royal Welch Fusiliers

Sussex £58,700 ($93,333)
26.III.97

Thomas Bernard Hackett was commissioned Ensign in the Royal Welch Fusiliers in June 1854 and the following year, upon promotion to Lieutenant, joined his regiment in the Crimea where he served in the siege of Sebastopol. In 1857 he took part in the suppression of the Indian Mutiny where he won his Victoria Cross on the outskirts of Lucknow as Sir Colin Campbell's force fought its way to the relief of the beleaguered Residency. Here he led the rescue of a Corporal who was lying wounded and exposed to heavy fire. After extensive further duty during the Great Mutiny his only other active service was in West Africa during the Ashantee War of 1873, by which time he had attained the rank of Lieutenant-Colonel. Retiring in 1874, he died six years later, killed 'by the explosion of his own gun'.

The Titanic-Carpathia Medal, 1912, presented to Fifth Officer Gustav J. Rath

Gold, height 3.92 cm (1½ in), width 3.5 cm (1⅜ in)
New York $55,000 (£33,700)
29.VII.97

This medal was commissioned by the 705 survivors of the most famous maritime disaster in history to be presented to the crew of the Carpathia, who rescued them. The medal shows the head of Neptune and two dolphins flanking the Carpathia, with an inscription on the reverse. Just fourteen medals are believed to have been struck in gold for the officers of the R.M.S. Carpathia, of which only six are recorded in contemporary accounts as having been preserved. It is believed that this medal is the first specimen to have come to auction. It achieved a world record for a twentieth-century commemorative medal.

ARMS AND ARMOUR

An Italian Parade Helmet
Filippo Negroli of Milan,
c. 1530–35
Height 29.2 cm (11½ in)
Sussex £114,288 ($187,320)
15.VII.97
From the Collections of the
Earls of Warwick

Filippo Negroli is widely
considered to be the greatest
embosser of armour that
ever lived. His reputation is
based on his masterly
handling of the material and
sense of design. In 1550
Giorgio Vasari praised his
skilful chiselling of leafwork
and figures on iron, while
Paolo Morigia in his *Nobilitá*

di Milano of 1595, observed
that 'Filippo Negroli
deserves undying praise, for
it is he who has been the
leading craftsman in working
on iron in relief and low
relief . . .'. This helmet can be
attributed to Negroli on the
basis of its very close
resemblance to two signed
examples of his work.

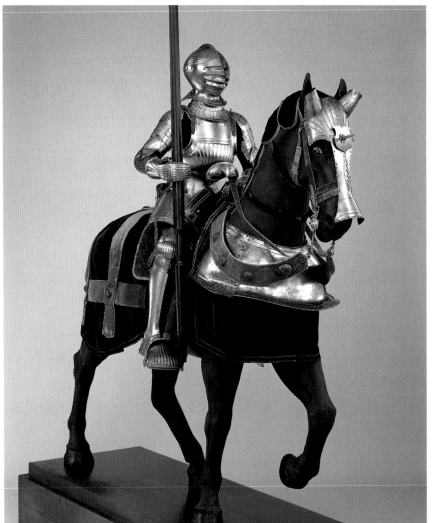

**A Composite Fluted Full
Armour Mounted with a
Light Horse Armour**
German, c. 1515–30
New York $233,500
(£144,770) 31.1.97
From the Metropolitan
Museum of Art, New York

This composed set of
armour is struck with the
Nuremberg guild mark on
a number of its elements.
Magnificently styled fluted
plate armour evolved as a
means of achieving
structural strength and
became prevalent
throughout the German
cultural sphere within the
first half of the sixteenth
century.

SPORTING GUNS

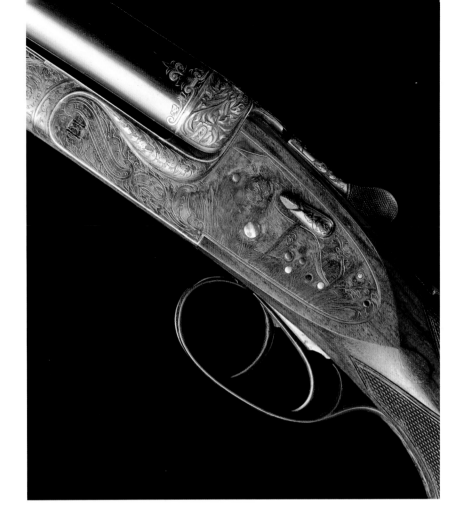

Holland & Holland
A .500/.465 Nitro Express Royal 'Modele de Luxe' Detachable Sidelock Ejector Rifle, No. 35289, 1955
Gleneagles £28,750
($47,150) 19.VIII.96

This highly decorated rifle is engraved with scrolls and detailed vignettes: the right lock depicts a charging rhinoceros in a landscape, the left lock shows a lion and the action base an advancing tiger. The gun appears unused and retains its original hardening colour and finish.

J. Purdey & Sons
A .306 Hammer Gun
No. 16774, 1899
London £34,500 ($55,911)
19.11.97

This gun was delivered by James Purdey & Sons on 21 December 1899 for HRH Prince Edward of York. The young prince wrote to Athol Purdey three days later from York Cottage, Sandringham, thanking him for the 'nice' gun and wishing him a happy new year. Edward was five-and-a-half years old when he received this gift. The highly figured stock with gold escutcheon is engraved with a crowned 'E'.

MUSICAL INSTRUMENTS

**Jacob and Abraham Kirckman
A Two-manual Harpsichord**
London, 1776
234 × 94.5 cm (7 ft 8 in ×
3 ft 1¼ in)
London £102,700 ($172,536)
21.XI.96

This five-octave harpsichord is decorated with extensive marquetry, including a musical trophy on the faciaboard, which is flanked by angel trumpeters and parrots. Ebony and ivory keys are accompanied by hand stops for both manuals. The legs of the harpsichord are carved at the knee with acanthus leaves, and end in claw-and-ball feet. The maker's initials appear on the soundboard, and the instrument is inscribed *Jacobus et Abraham Kirckman fecerunt Londini 1776.*

**Giovanni Battista Guadagnini
A Violin**
Turin, *c.* 1775
Length of back 35.3 cm
(13⅞ in)
London £243,500 ($401,775)
5.XI.96

This wonderfully preserved example of Guadagnini's later years is labelled *Jo. Bapt. Guadagnini Cremonensis alumnus Antonii Stradivari fecit Taurini . . . .* As Guadagnini was not actually born in Cremona, nor a pupil of Stradivari, the label is evidence of his respect for Stradivari's work rather than any direct link with his famous predecessor. Stradivari's influence is clear in the flatness of the arch, the cut of the f-holes and the glorious orange varnish.

VINTAGE AND VETERAN CARS

**1930 Duesenberg Model J
Convertible Victoria**
New York $662,500
(£424,000) 5.x.96
From the Collection of
Andrew D. Darling

A one-off commission, this
Duesenberg Model J was
constructed in Paris to a
design by Howard Darrin; it
was then shipped to America
by its owner, Mrs Honoree
Palmer, in 1934. Bought by
Andrew Darling in 1970, the
car was in need of a total
restoration and this was
carried out by the best
restorer of the time, Culver
Beaver. The car is finished in
burgundy lacquer with cream
pinstriping; its interior is
trimmed in biscuit leather
with tan carpets and it is
fitted with a tan Haartz
cloth top.

**1927 Rolls-Royce Phantom I
Brougham de Ville**
London £67,500 ($110,025)
14.VI.97

Luxury cars of the utmost
variety and interest were
produced throughout the
vintage decade of the
twenties, as is clear from this
version of the Phantom I.
Henri Binder, established
in Paris as coachbuilders
from the turn of the century,
were responsible for the
fashionable coachwork, and
the stylish 'Motor Brougham'
closely resembled its horse-
drawn predecessor with
highly stylized angular lines
and exposure of the
chauffeur's compartment.
This example was first owned
by Mrs James Donahue, the
Woolworth heiress.

WINE

A Selection of Bottles, Magnums and One Double Magnum of Château Cheval Blanc

London £14,487 ($23,324)
19.11.97

The great St Emilion Premier Grand Cru Classé Cheval Blanc featured in some of its finest vintages in this sale. The opulent character of Cheval Blanc showed to perfection in years from 1959 to 1985, including the highly sought-after 1982. Cheval Blanc is a wine that tastes beautifully at all stages of its life, whether young and vibrant or mature and velvety.

A Bottle of Jefferson Madeira 1800

New York $23,000 (£14,030)
16.v.97

Madeira is the longest lived of all wines, and the exceptional provenance of this bottle makes it of enormous historic importance. Once belonging to President Thomas Jefferson, it was handed down through generations of an aristocratic family. The handwritten label states 'Jefferson Madeira 1800; purchased at sale of effects; President Jefferson; by Honl. Philip Evan Thomas of Maryland 1843; purchased at sale of effects; Mrs John Wethered, his daughter, April 1890; Douglas H. Thomas, filtered 1890'.

COLLECTIBLES

The Copy of the Jules Rimet Cup Used as the World Cup Football Trophy Between 1968 and 1970
c. 1968, English
Gilded bronze
Height 33 cm (13 in)
London £254,500 ($430,105)
11.VII.97

The Football Association commissioned this copy of the Jules Rimet Cup following the theft of the original in 1966. Found by a dog called Pickles, the original was thereafter kept in the company safe, while the copy was used for promotions and exhibitions. That this cup was a copy was a closely guarded secret, and it was always heavily guarded while on public view. The original cup was stolen again after being sent to Brazil, and has not been seen since; this is the only exact replica of the original in existence.

The Mummy
1932, Universal
104.1 × 68.6 cm (41 × 27 in)
New York $453,500
(£276,635) 1.III.97

The Mummy, starring Boris Karloff, is considered to be one of the classic horror films of the 1930s. This is one of only two known copies of the one-sheet poster which was illustrated by Karoly Grosz, Universal's advertising art director throughout the thirties. Grosz produced posters for most of Universal's horror classics, which are now highly coveted by collectors.

**The Cowardly Lion
Courage Medal from
*The Wizard of Oz***

1939
19.1 × 19.1 cm (7½ × 7½ in),
framed 38.2 × 30.5 cm
(15 × 12 in)
Beverly Hills $33,350
(£20,010) 21.v.97

This medal, originally
presented to the Cowardly
Lion by the Wizard of Oz in
the film of the same name,
was given to Mal Caplan by
his colleagues at MGM in the
late 1950s. Caplan, who had
worked his way up from
floor-sweeper to head of the
costume department, had
been very badly injured in a
car accident and, unable to
sit up, had to work from a
chaise longue for some time.
In recognition of his fortitude,
his workmates had the
medal framed and captioned
'Mal Caplan, Keep Smiling,
Keep Calm, Keep Cool'.

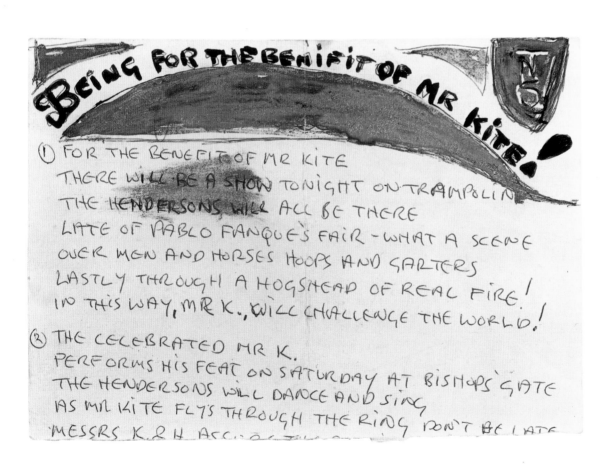

**John Lennon's
Handwritten Lyrics to
'Being For the Benefit Of
Mr Kite!'**

1967
13.5 × 19 cm (5¼ × 7½ in)
London £66,400 ($103,584)
19.ix.96

Appearing on *Sergeant
Pepper's Lonely Heart's Club
Band*, widely considered as
the most influential rock
album of all time, this
composition was inspired by
the acts featured on a
Victorian circus poster that
Lennon found in an antiques
shop. The incomplete set of
lyrics are written in blue
ballpoint pen with the song's
title highlighted in black ink
and gold paint; Lennon's
working notes are in pencil
on the reverse. The price
achieved was a new world
record for Lennon lyrics.

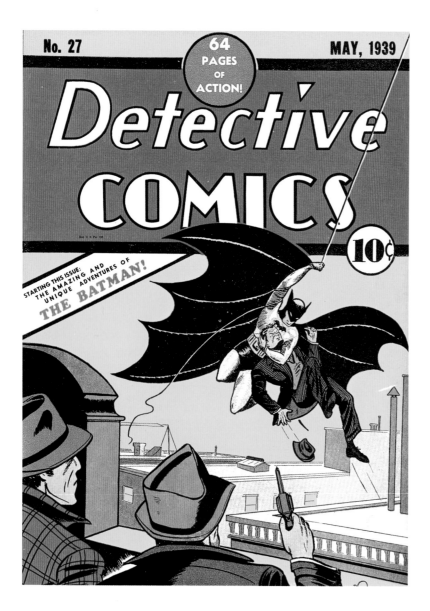

Detective Comics No. 27
May 1939, National
Periodical Publications
New York $68,500 (£41,785)
13.VI.97

There are more than fifty
copies of this comic book in
existence, but only three are
in near-mint condition, and
this is the finest unrestored
issue ever offered for public
sale. This copy was offered
for sale at the first Sotheby's
Comic Books and Comic Art
auction in 1991.

**Celluloid from *Alice in
Wonderland***
1951, Walt Disney Studio
24.1 × 33 cm (9½ × 13 in)
New York $35,650 (£21,390)
14.XII.96

This celluloid is from the
scene in Walt Disney's *Alice
in Wonderland* where Alice
comes across the hookah-
smoking caterpillar. Here she
is talking to the red rose, as a
tulip and blue foxglove look
on. The scene is executed
in gouache on a trimmed
celluloid, applied to a
trimmed watercolour
production background
from a scene in Tuggley
Woods. The mat is signed
on the lower right 'To C.
McGivern, with best wishes,
Walt Disney'.

Machine Man
Masudaya, 1950s
Height 38.1 cm (15 in)
New York $42,550 (£25,955)
7.XI.96
From the Collection of
Matt Wyse

This is one of only three
known examples of the
Machine Man from the Gang
of Five series. He has battery-
powered green lighting eyes,
ears and mouth, and a
bump-and-go action with
moving arms. He is finished
in red with lithographed
decorative panels. This
example set a new world
auction record for a robot.

**A Roullet et Decamps
Musical Automaton of
a Snake Charmer**
French, c. 1900
90 cm (35¾ in)
London £155,500 ($245,690)
17.X.96
From the Dina Vierny
Collection

With a serpent in her left
hand and a trumpet in her
right, when activated, this
figure alternately lifts the
objects towards her face. She
has moving eyelids, and
sways her head in time to the
four tunes played by the
mechanism in the base. The
maker was able to leave her
arm bare, as he concealed its
articulation within her
jewellery. She was based on
'Zulma' the Snake Charmer,
an act performed at the
Folies-Bergères in Paris in
the 1890s.

An Evening Gown

Norman Norell
1960s, *NORMAN NORELL,*
NEW YORK on white label
Size US 8
New York $8,625 (£5,261)
8.IV.97
Property from the Estate of
Martha Phillips

This sleeveless, empire-
waisted floor-length tunic
dress is tied with a black
satin sash. The satin tunic
with netting is covered with
a myriad of small, clear
rhinestone jewels falling to
below the knee then forming
a large band of bugle-beaded
silvery crystal flowers,
terminating in a bugle-bead
fringe. This was a record for
a Norell dress.

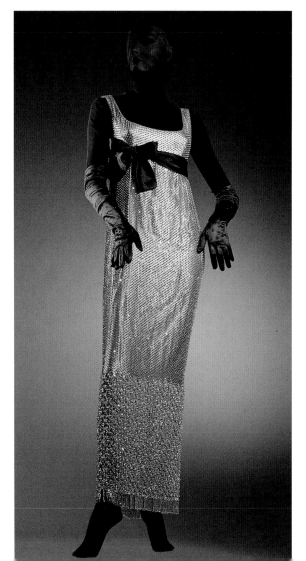

A Polychrome Needlepoint and Lace Sampler

English, *c.* 1650–70
36 × 23.5 cm (14⅛ × 9¼ in)
in wooden frame
London £62,000 ($99,200)
13.III.97

This sampler is worked in
five distinct bands, two with
figures, one showing a
mermaid and merman with a
ship and another possibly
depicting Susannah and the
Elders. Parts of the sampler
have seed pearls and coral
beads as additional
decoration. The condition

and depth of colour of the
piece reflect the fact that it
was stored rolled up in a
drawer and was only framed
recently. It is believed to be
the most extensive and
complex polychrome
needlepoint and lace
sampler in existence.

A Hand-painted Wooden Noah's Ark

German, *c.* 1840
Length 65 cm (25½ in)
London £22,425 ($36,777)
4.VI.97

This ark, with 250 animals, insects and figures, was owned by one family from the 1850s until it was sold in 1997. The inscription inside reads 'Presented to the Revd John Edwards MA about 1854 at Todmorden For his five children'. The ark has a sliding wooden door, sixteen painted windows, a painted door and flower borders. The pitched roof has a painted tile effect and a painted dove. The animals are individually labelled.

A J. Moxon Royal Presentation Pocket Globe

English, *c.* 1690
7.5 cm (3 in) diameter
London £62,000 ($99,820)
7.III.97

Joseph Moxon (1627–91) was the originator of the pocket globe, an object that became hugely popular in the eighteenth and early nineteenth centuries. This example has a sharkskin case, containing a hand-coloured print of the constellations on its interior and the royal monograms of William and Mary on the exterior. The globe shows California as an island, and is similar to one Moxon made for Queen Anne to present to Frederick I, King of Prussia.

Syon Park, Middlesex

In May 1997 Sotheby's sold works of art collected by three great English families – the Percys, Dukes of Northumberland and Lords Warkworth; the Grevilles, Earls of Warwick and Lords Brooke; and the Barons Methuen. All three families were already collecting works of art in the seventeenth century and continued into the twentieth century. Typically of such great family collections, their houses were filled with the expected: Old Master paintings, silver, furniture and porcelain, and the unexpected: painted tapestries, Portuguese furniture and German silver.

The sale was held in the grounds of the great Thames-side country house, Syon Park, the London residence of the Duke of Northumberland. Originally a monastery, Syon Park was granted to the Dukes of Somerset after the Reformation in the sixteenth century. Thereafter it oscillated by inheritance between the Seymours and Percys for the next two hundred years. Lady Elizabeth Seymour inherited Syon Park in 1750 and clearly intended to use Syon for entertaining immediately. Together with her husband Hugh, 1st Duke of Northumberland, she commissioned Andien de Clermont to paint a series of decorative murals (*right*), and later employed Robert Adam, who created a series of magnificent neo-classical rooms for entertaining.

Amongst the highlights of the sale was the George IV silver-gilt Warwick vase, which was sold for almost double its estimated price. The vase is a replica of the marble original, fragments of which were found at Hadrian's villa near Rome in 1770. The original was restored, then bought by George Greville, 2nd Earl of Warwick and was on display in Warwick Castle by 1774. Through an engraving by Piranesi and a description published in the *Gentleman's Magazine* in 1800, the vase became well known, and a variety of objects copying the design were made. This silver-gilt version was presented to Sir Charles Greville, KCB, the second son of the 2nd Earl of Warwick, by his regiment. Other items of particular interest from the sale were the reduction of the monument to Marshall Blücher, the Prussian war hero from the Battle of Waterloo in 1815, and the ebony bedhead with its marine theme, bought by Henry, 3rd Earl of Warwick in about 1830.

Andien de Clermont
A Painted Canvas
'Singeries' Mural
c. 1750, distemper on canvas
338 × 285 cm (11 ft × 9 ft 2 in)
Syon Park, Middlesex
£32,200 ($52,808) 14.v.97
The Property of the 10th
Duke of Northumberland's
Will Trust

**Christian Daniel Rauch
A Berlin Cast-iron Reduction
of the Monument to
Marshall Blücher at Breslau**
c. 1825
Height 147.5 cm (58 in)
Syon Park, Middlesex
£62,000 ($101,680) 14.v.97
Sold by the Executors of the
Rt. Hon John, 6th Baron
Methuen

**Philip Rundell for Rundell,
Bridge and Rundell, London
A George IV Silver-gilt
Warwick Vase, 1821**
Diameter 27.5 cm (11 in)
Syon Park, Middlesex
£20,700 ($33,948) 15.v.97
From the Collections of the
Earls of Warwick

**An Indo-Portuguese Ebony
Tester Bedhead**
18th century
Ebony, ivory and tortoiseshell,
287 × 185.5 × 211 cm (9 ft 5 in
× 6 ft 1 in × 6 ft 11 in)
Syon Park, Middlesex
£111,500 ($182,860) 14.v.97
From the Collections of the
Earls of Warwick

PRINCIPAL OFFICERS AND SPECIALISTS

Diana D. Brooks
President and Chief Executive Officer, Board of Directors, Sotheby's Holdings, Inc.

Simon de Pury
Chairman, Board of Directors, Sotheby's Europe and Sotheby's Switzerland

Henry Wyndham
Chairman, Sotheby's UK

John L. Marion
Honorary Chairman, Sotheby's North America

Richard Oldenburg
Chairman, Sotheby's North America

Alice Lam
Co-Chairman, Management Board, Sotheby's Asia

Julian Thompson
Co-Chairman, Management Board, Sotheby's Asia

George Bailey
Managing Director, Sotheby's Europe

William F. Ruprecht
Managing Director, Sotheby's North America

American Decorative Arts & Furniture
Wendell Garrett
New York 606 7137
Leslie B. Keno
New York 606 7130
William W. Stahl, Jnr
New York 606 7110

American Folk Art
Nancy Druckman
New York 606 7225

American Indian Art
Ellen Napiura Taubman
New York 606 7540

American Paintings, Drawings & Sculpture
Dara Mitchell
New York 606 7280
Peter B. Rathbone
New York 606 7280

Animation & Comic Art
Jon Baddeley
London 408 5205
Dana Hawkes
New York 606 7910

Antiquities & Indian Art
Marcus Fraser
London 408 5332
Richard M. Keresey
(*antiquities*)
New York 606 7328
Carlton Rochell (*Indian*)
New York 606 7304

Applied Arts from 1850
Barbara E. Deisroth
New York 606 7170
Philippe Garner
London 408 5138

Arms, Armour & Medals
Nicholas McCulloch
Sussex 783933
Margaret Schwartz
New York 606 7250

Art
Alexander Apsis
New York 606 7352
Melanie Clore
London 408 5394
Philip Hook
London 408 5223
Andrew Strauss
Paris 53 05 53 55
Michel Strauss
London 408 5403
John L. Tancock
New York 606 7360

Books & Manuscripts
Paul Needham
New York 606 7385
Christina Orobetz
Toronto 926 1774
David N. Redden
New York 606 7386
Dr Stephen Roe
London 408 5286

British Paintings 1500–1850
David Moore-Gwyn
London 408 5406
James Miller
London 408 5405
Henry Wemyss
(*watercolours*)
London 408 5409

British Paintings from 1850
Martin Gallon (*Victorian*)
London 408 5386
Susannah Pollen (*20th century*)
London 408 5388
Simon Taylor (*Victorian*)
London 408 5385

Canadian Art
Christina Orobetz
Toronto 926 1774

Ceramics
Peter Arney
London 408 5134
Letitia Roberts
New York 606 7180

Chinese Art
James B. Godfrey
New York 606 7332
Noah Kupferman
New York 606 7334
Colin Mackay
London 408 5145
Julian Thompson
London 408 5371

Clocks & Watches
Tina Millar (*watches*)
London 408 5328
Daryn Schnipper
New York 606 7162
Michael Turner (*clocks*)
London 408 5329

Coins
Tom Eden (*ancient & Islamic*)
London 408 5313
James Morton (*English & paper money*)
London 408 5314
Paul Song
New York 606 7856

Collector's Department
Dana Hawkes
New York 606 7910
Hilary Kay
London 408 5020

Contemporary Art
Florence de Botton
Paris 53 05 53 60
Elena Geuna
London 408 5401
Tobias Meyer
New York 606 7254
Leslie Prouty
New York 606 7254

English Furniture & Decorations
Graham Child
London 408 5347
Joseph Friedman
London 408 5474
Larry J. Sirolli
New York 606 7577
William W. Stahl, Jnr
New York 606 7110

European Works of Art
Margaret Schwartz
New York 606 7250
Elizabeth Wilson
London 408 5321

Fashion
Tiffany Dubin
New York 606 7263

French & Continental Furniture & Decorations
Phillips Hathaway
New York 606 7213
Thierry Millerand
New York 606 7213
Alexandre Pradère
Paris 53 05 53 00
Mario Tavella
London 408 5052

Garden Statuary & Architectural Items
James Rylands
Sussex 783239
London 408 5073
Elaine Whitmire
New York 606 7285

Glass & Paperweights
Simon Cottle
London 408 5133
Lauren K. Tarshis
New York 606 7180

Islamic Art & Carpets
Jacqueline Coulter (*carpets*)
London 408 5152
Marcus Fraser (*works of art*)
London 408 5332
Richard M. Keresey (*works of art*)
New York 606 7328
Mary Jo Otsea (*carpets*)
New York 606 7996

Japanese Art
Neil Davey
London 408 5141
Gretchen Good
New York 606 7338
Ryoichi Iida
New York 606 7338

Jewellery
David Bennett
Geneva 908 4840
John D. Block
New York 606 7535
Lisa Hubbard
Los Angeles 274 0340
Alexandra Rhodes
London 408 5311

Judaica
David Breuer-Weil
Tel Aviv 522 38 22
Paul Needham (*books*)
New York 606 7385
Camilla Previté
London 408 5334
Kevin Tierney (*silver*)
New York 606 7160

Korean Works of Art
Ryoichi Iida
New York 606 7338
Jiyoung Koo
New York 606 7286

Latin American Art
Isabella Hutchinson
New York 606 7290

Musical Instruments
Rachel Gaul
New York 606 7938
Graham Wells
London 408 5341

19th Century European Furniture & Works of Art
Jonathan Meyer
London 408 5350
Elaine Whitmire
New York 606 7285

19th Century European Paintings & Drawings
Michael Bing
London 408 5380
Benjamin Doller
New York 606 7140
Nancy Harrison
New York 606 7140
Rob Mulders
Amsterdam 550 2263
Pascale Pavageau
Paris 53 05 53 10

Old Master Paintings & Drawings
Alexander Bell
London 408 5420
Frédéric Gourd
Paris 53 05 53 10
Gregory Rubinstein (*drawings*)
London 408 5417
Scott Schaefer (*drawings*)
New York 606 7230
Julien Stock
Rome 669 41791
George Wachter
New York 606 7230

Oriental Manuscripts
Marcus Fraser
London 408 5332
Carlton Rochell
New York 606 7304

Photographs
Denise Bethel
New York 606 7240
Philippe Garner
London 408 5138

Portrait Miniatures & Objects of Vertu
Heinrich Graf von Spreti
Munich 2909 5121
Gerald Hill
New York 606 7150
Haydn Williams
London 408 5326

Postage Stamps
Richard Ashton
London 408 5224
Robert A.G.A. Scott
New York 606 7915

Pre-Columbian Art
Stacy Goodman
New York 606 7330
Fatma Turkkan-Wille
Zürich 422 3045

Prints
Mary Bartow (*19th & 20th century*)
New York 606 7117
Nancy Bialler (*Old Master*)
New York 606 7117
Jonathan Pratt
London 408 5212
Nina del Rio (*contemporary*)
New York 606 7113

Russian Paintings & Icons
Michael Bing
London 408 5380
Gerard Hill
New York 606 7150

Silver
Harold Charteris (*Continental*)
London 408 5106
Ian Irving
New York 606 7160
Kobus du Plessis
Paris 53 05 53 20
Kevin L. Tierney
New York 606 7160
Peter Waldron (*English*)
London 408 5104

Sporting Guns
Adrian Wellar
Sussex 783241

Tribal Art
Jean G. Fritts
New York 606 7325

Vintage Cars
Martin Chisholm
London 408 5320
David Partridge
New York 606 7920

Western Manuscripts
Dr Christopher de Hamel, FSA
London 408 5330

Wine
Jamie Ritchie
New York 606 7523
Serena Sutcliffe
London 408 5050

Sotheby's World Wide Web Site
http://www.sothebys.com

INDEX

Acknowledgements

Prices given throughout include the buyer's premium applicable in the saleroom concerned. These prices are shown in the currency in which they were realized. The sterling and dollar equivalent figures, shown in brackets, are based upon the rates of exchange on the day of the sale.

The editor would like to thank Ronald Varney, Suzanne McMillan, Luke Rittner, William F. Ruprecht, Ken Adlard, Susanne Waugh, Sidney Long, Jadwiga Gromadzka, Emma Fraser and all the Sotheby's departments for their help with this book.

Photographic Acknowledgements
The editor would like to thank the following photographers and organizations for their kind permission to reproduce the photographs in the book:
© ADAGP, Paris and DACS, London 1997 71, 83, 95, 96
Ken Adlard/Sotheby's 8, 16 (top left), 22, 31 (top & bottom left), 34
© ARS, New York and DACS, London 1997 87, 90, 104, 116
Pascal Blancon/Sotheby's 16 (bottom left)
© DACS 1997 31, 32, 84, 93
Dominic Garner 33 (bottom)
Leslie Jean-Bart/Sotheby's 13, 18, 26, 28, 36, 250
© Jasper Johns/VAGA, New York/DACS, London 1997 117
© Munch Museum/Munch-Ellingsen Group, Oslo/DACS, London 1997 80, 114
Richard Pearson 38
© Succession H Matisse/DACS 1997 115